RUNNING
MADE
SIMPLE

A Beginner's Guide to Jogging and the Basics of Running

Shawn Tunis

First Edition

Published by Shawn Tunis

Table Of Contents

Introduction

Embarking on a journey into the world of jogging and running is a transformative step toward enhancing your physical fitness, mental well-being, and overall health. This beginner's guide is designed to be your companion, providing essential insights into the fundamentals of jogging and running, irrespective of your current fitness level. Whether you're taking your initial strides or transitioning from walking to jogging or jogging to running, this guide aims to demystify the basics, offer valuable tips, and inspire you to embrace the joy and benefits that jogging and running can bring to your life.

We've all heard the phrases:

- "I hate running."
- "Running is a form of punishment, right?"

Sound familiar? Or you may have said one or all of these yourself.

Let me share a little secret with you: The majority of passionate recreational runners initially had the same thoughts.

What happened to them?

Small strides. To tap into the extensive physical and emotional advantages that running offers, one must begin with small, baby steps.

Alright, maybe running to the mailbox may even be tough for you. And? There are plenty of marathoners who couldn't do that either.

I'm not suggesting you have to run a marathon. Everyone's goals are different. There are a multitude of factors that drive runners to become incredibly devoted or perhaps even addicted.

At first, understanding the advantages and pleasures of running might be challenging, but once grasped, it becomes hard to let go.

As the ancient Chinese philosopher Lao Tze stated, "The journey of 1000 miles begins with one step." Let's start by walking to the mailbox, then progress to jogging, and finally, running!

So if you're ready to start a new journey and tap into the extensive physical and emotional advantages to come, let's delve into the exhilarating world of jogging and running collectively.

Welcome to **Running Made Simple: "A Beginner's Guide to Jogging and the Basics of Running."**

Chapter 1: Running or Jogging: What's the Difference?

While some individuals find satisfaction in jogging, others are content with running or brisk walking. So, what sets running apart from jogging? The primary distinction lies in the rhythmic and controlled pace of jogging compared to the often less rhythmic nature of running. A jogger typically maintains a steady pace throughout the entire activity, while a runner may slow down or even come to a halt every few miles. This divergence can be attributed to the jogger's ability to sustain a consistent, slower pace, in contrast to the runner who often starts slow, accelerates, and then decelerates or stops when unable to maintain that initial pace.

Here's a closer look at the unique attributes of jogging and running.

Jogging is a moderate-intensity aerobic exercise that falls between walking and running in terms of pace. It involves a gentle bounce or trot, usually at a pace faster than walking but slower than running. Jogging is an excellent cardiovascular workout that helps improve stamina, endurance, and overall cardiovascular health. It is often chosen by individuals seeking a middle-ground option that provides a more intense workout than walking without the impact associated with running.

Running is a higher-intensity form of aerobic exercise characterized by a faster pace and a more dynamic movement pattern than jogging. It involves a flight phase, where both feet are off the ground simultaneously. Running offers numerous health benefits, including improved cardiovascular fitness, enhanced muscular strength, and increased calorie burn. It is a popular choice for those looking to challenge themselves physically and engage in a more intense workout.

The crucial aspect is to engage in activities that feel comfortable for you. If you're aiming to establish a consistent exercise routine, starting with jogging might be more suitable than running. This doesn't imply that running is unfavorable, but jogging may offer a more sustainable long-term exercise routine, especially for beginners. Maintaining a steady pace is more effective than frequently altering your speed, which is particularly significant for individuals who may find it challenging to sustain running or jogging for extended periods

Opting for a consistent pace during your jogging routine will assist in maintaining a steady heart rate and prevent you from feeling breathless or overexerted. Maintaining a consistent pace is healthier than either moving too quickly or frequently altering your speed, which can lead to an elevated heart rate and the onset of cramps.

If you find pleasure in both running and jogging, consider alternating between the two to diversify your routine. Keep in mind that you may have greater endurance during your jogging sessions, so reserve running for moments when you feel particularly energetic. Morning runs before work can be invigorating, although a leisurely jog is also a valid choice. The key is not the specific activity—whether running or jogging—but ensuring you safeguard your feet with properly fitting shoes designed for the chosen activity. Additionally, prioritize regularly replacing your athletic shoes instead of waiting until they are worn out. Opt for moisture-wicking materials in your clothing to stay dry and comfortable during your jogging sessions.

A common error people often commit is persisting in jogging despite feeling pain in their knees or legs. It's crucial to stop if you're experiencing pain, as pushing through it may lead to more severe consequences later on.

In the course of this book, you may find the terms jogging and running used interchangeably or in combination. Don't be perplexed; if you identify as a jogger, you are also a runner. Let's get started!

Is There a Right or Wrong Way to Jog?

A valid and straightforward question, isn't it? How does one properly jog? Is there a definitive right or wrong way to jog? While some may argue that it doesn't make a significant difference, opinions on this matter may vary. Personal preferences play a key role, and when these preferences deviate from the practices of others, they might be perceived as "wrong." Is that an absolute truth? Not necessarily. However, from the perspective of someone engaging in a different approach, it might indeed seem like an incorrect way of carrying out a particular activity. Whether it involves jogging, running, or even mundane tasks like vacuuming the floor, some individuals believe there exists a proper and improper way to do it.

Looking back, jogging entails a gradual and rhythmic movement resembling a run, more akin to a trot or gallop, rather than a full-fledged run. Due to its slower tempo, individuals who may not be able to run often find jogging accessible. However, this isn't universally applicable, as exceptions exist, such as for heart patients or those limited to brisk or leisurely walks. For those fortunate enough to enjoy jogging, they tend to develop their own unique approach, with no inherently right or wrong way to do it. The primary focus lies in maintaining a slow, steady pace, and aside from that, there's no absolute right or wrong method, except in the minds of some perfectionists.

Regardless of the guidance people receive about jogging, they inevitably develop their own approach, one that suits them best. The decision is deeply personal, and as long as the outcome aligns, the reasoning or methodology that distinguishes one person's style from another holds little significance. Jogging methods will naturally vary based on individual preferences, weight, and body build. Some individuals find specific jogging styles more comfortable, with some even opting to switch between jogging, brisk walking, and running. The impact on your health is not determined by your jogging style but rather by your commitment to the activity. Opting for jogging as your preferred exercise to maintain good health will likely contribute to a longer and healthier life compared to those who choose a sedentary lifestyle.

Chapter 2: The Benefits of Jogging

Jogging is a popular form of exercise that offers numerous benefits for people of all ages and fitness levels. Whether you are a beginner or an experienced runner, incorporating jogging into your routine can have a positive impact on your physical and mental well-being. In this chapter, we will explore the various benefits of jogging and why it is a fantastic choice for individuals seeking an enjoyable and effective exercise option.

Maintaining good health requires regular exercise, and that doesn't necessarily entail spending hours in a gym every week. For those who aren't inclined towards gym workouts, daily jogging can be an ideal exercise routine. It effectively achieves the intended goals of boosting the heart rate and metabolism. Even if your weight falls within the normal range, it's beneficial to engage in an exercise routine that accelerates your metabolism to help sustain a healthy weight. Of course, if weight loss is your goal, creating a calorie deficit by burning more calories than you consume becomes essential.

While it might appear inconsequential to individuals without weight concerns, exercise holds significant importance. To sustain good health, it's crucial to engage in activities that elevate the heart rate and enhance calorie burning. Even without a rise in food consumption, neglecting to burn the calories you ingest can lead to weight gain. This is a common source of confusion for individuals who wonder why they're gaining weight despite not increasing their food intake—leading a sedentary lifestyle limits the opportunity for calorie expenditure.

A notable advantage of jogging is its impact on weight management. As a high-energy activity, jogging efficiently burns calories, making it a superb option for individuals aiming to lose weight or sustain a healthy weight. Beyond the immediate calorie expenditure during the activity, jogging also elevates your metabolic rate, resulting in a sustained calorie burn even after completing your run.

Another additional advantage, which may not be immediately evident to everyone, is that engaging consistently in an exercise routine like jogging tends to heighten awareness of dietary choices. Instead of lounging around and snacking on chips or other unhealthy foods, there's a greater inclination to opt for nutritious choices. It might be a subconscious effect, but exercise appears to make individuals more mindful of what they consume. While this isn't universally true for everyone, a substantial number of people do find themselves subconsciously making healthier food choices when they commit to regular exercise.

Jogging also serves as an excellent method for enhancing cardiovascular health. Consistent jogging contributes to the strengthening of heart muscles, the expansion of lung capacity, and the improvement of blood circulation throughout the body. Consequently, this can decrease the risk of heart disease, high blood pressure, and stroke. Furthermore, research indicates that jogging can reduce levels of bad cholesterol and elevate levels of good cholesterol, providing additional support for a healthier cardiovascular system.

Jogging also exerts a beneficial influence on mental health. Consistent jogging triggers the release of endorphins, natural mood enhancers that effectively alleviate stress, anxiety, and symptoms of depression. For numerous joggers, a run serves as a type of meditation, enabling them to declutter their minds and attain a sense of peace and tranquility. Furthermore, jogging outdoors offers a chance to connect with nature and appreciate the beauty of the surroundings, adding an extra layer to the enhancement of mental well-being.

Furthermore, jogging is a low-cost and accessible form of exercise. All you need is a good pair of running shoes, and you can jog almost anywhere at any time. Whether it's a local park, a neighborhood street, or a treadmill at home, jogging offers the convenience of being able to exercise whenever and wherever it suits you.

How often should you jog? It's a personal choice, but ideally, aim for a duration of at least thirty to forty-five minutes daily. If a continuous block of time is challenging, consider breaking it into intervals of fifteen to twenty minutes. For those who utilize their lunch break for exercise, it's crucial to note that even shorter jogs necessitate wearing properly fitting and suitable shoes to prevent potential damage to your feet, legs, and knees.

Regardless of whether you are a novice jogger or an experienced runner, never underestimate the importance of a thorough warm-up and cool-down. Dedicate time to ready your body and mind before each run, and you'll enjoy the advantages of a safer, more effective, and rewarding jogging experience.

In summary, jogging presents a plethora of advantages suitable for individuals at various fitness levels. Whether it's enhancing cardiovascular health, aiding in weight management, promoting mental well-being, or serving as a budget-friendly exercise option, jogging stands out as a fantastic choice for those seeking an effective and enjoyable way to maintain fitness. So, strap on your running shoes, hit the pavement, and discover the myriad benefits of jogging firsthand.

Setting Goals for Your Running Journey

Whether you are a seasoned runner or just starting out on your jogging journey, setting goals is one of the most important aspects of achieving success. Goals provide direction, motivation, and a sense of accomplishment, helping you stay focused and committed to your running routine. In this subchapter, we will explore the significance of setting goals for your running journey and provide you with practical tips to help you get started.

First and foremost, setting goals allows you to define what you want to achieve with your running. Are you looking to improve your overall fitness, run your first 5K race, or perhaps complete a marathon? Whatever your aspirations may be, having a clear goal in mind will help you create a plan and structure your training accordingly.

When setting goals, it's essential to ensure they are specific, measurable, attainable, relevant, and time-bound (SMART). Instead of a broad objective like "improving at running," consider setting a goal such as completing a 5K race in under 40 minutes within the next three months. This specific target allows for progress tracking and helps maintain motivation throughout your running endeavors.

It's crucial to establish both short-term and long-term goals. Short-term objectives offer immediate satisfaction and motivation, while long-term goals help maintain focus on the broader perspective. Begin with achievable short-term goals, such as running continuously for 30 minutes, and progressively advance to more ambitious long-term goals, such as completing a half marathon.

Additionally, setting goals allows you to celebrate your achievements along the way. As you accomplish each milestone, take the time to acknowledge your progress and reward yourself. Recognizing your accomplishments will boost your confidence and keep you motivated to continue pushing yourself further.

Remember, your running journey is unique to you, and your goals should reflect that. Be realistic about your abilities and take into consideration your current fitness level and lifestyle. Setting overly ambitious goals can lead to frustration and disappointment, whereas setting attainable goals will provide you with a sense of accomplishment and inspire you to keep going.

To sum up, establishing goals is fundamental for a thriving running journey. It provides direction, motivation, and a clear sense of purpose. Through the setting of specific, measurable, attainable, relevant, and time-bound goals—both short-term and long-term—you can monitor your progress, sustain motivation, and rejoice in your accomplishments along the path. So, lace up your running shoes, define your goals, and embark on an exhilarating adventure toward a healthier and more fit version of yourself!

Essential Gear for Jogging

When it comes to jogging, the proper gear can significantly impact your comfort, performance, and overall enjoyment of the activity. Whether you're just starting out or an experienced runner, the investment in appropriate equipment is crucial. In this section, we'll delve into the essential gear necessary to ensure your jogging experience is safe, efficient, and enjoyable.

1. Running Shoes: The foundation of any runner's gear is a good pair of running shoes. Look for shoes that provide proper cushioning, support, and a comfortable fit. Consider visiting a specialty running store to get fitted for the right pair based on your foot type and running style.

2. Moisture-Wicking Clothing: Choose clothing made from moisture-wicking materials that will keep you dry and comfortable during your jog. Avoid cotton as it tends to retain moisture and can lead to chafing and discomfort.

3. Sports Bra (for women): Women should invest in a high-quality sports bra that provides adequate support and minimizes bounce. Look for bras specifically designed for running to ensure maximum comfort and reduce potential breast tissue damage. A quality sports bra with a good sturdy bra shelf is a good investment.

4. Socks: Opt for moisture-wicking socks made from synthetic materials or merino wool. These types of socks will help prevent blisters and keep your feet dry and comfortable. Bombas socks is a great, reputable brand for running socks. They've created the most comfortable socks you could imagine. And for every sock you purchase, a sock of the same kind is donated to those experiencing homelessness.

5. GPS Watch/Smartphone: Consider investing in a GPS watch or use a running app on your smartphone to track your distance, pace, and other important metrics. This will help you monitor your progress and set achievable goals. An Apple Watch will suffice. A more training-specific brand is Garmin.

6. Reflective Gear: If you plan on jogging during low-light conditions, such as early mornings or evenings, invest in reflective gear to make yourself more visible to motorists. This can include reflective vests, armbands, or even a headlamp.

7. Hydration Accessories: Staying hydrated is crucial during any workout. Carry a water bottle or invest in a hydration belt or backpack to ensure you have access to water throughout your jog.

8. Sun Protection: Protect yourself from the sun's harmful rays by wearing a hat, sunglasses, and applying sunscreen before heading out for a jog. This will help prevent sunburn and reduce the risk of skin cancer.

By investing in the essential gear mentioned above, you'll be well-prepared for a safe and enjoyable jogging experience. Remember, it's important to find what works best for you, so don't hesitate to try different brands and styles until you find the perfect fit. Happy jogging!

Warm-up and Cool-down Techniques

In the world of running, warm-up and cool-down techniques are often overlooked but play a crucial role in preventing injuries and enhancing overall performance. Whether you are a seasoned runner or just starting out, incorporating these techniques into your running routine is essential for a safe and successful jogging experience.

A warm-up is a vital step before any physical activity. It prepares your body for the upcoming workout by gradually increasing your heart rate, improving blood flow to your muscles, and loosening up your joints. A proper warm-up session typically lasts for about 5-10 minutes and includes light aerobic exercises such as brisk walking, slow jogging, or cycling. These low-intensity activities gradually raise your body temperature, making your muscles more pliable and less prone to strains or sprains during your run.

Moreover, warm-up exercises can also help mentally prepare you for the run ahead. They allow you to focus on your breathing, stride, and form, helping you enter a zone of concentration and mindfulness. Remember, a good warm-up not only benefits your physical body but also sets the stage for a more enjoyable and productive jogging experience.

Stretching exercises during the cool-down phase are particularly beneficial for maintaining flexibility and reducing muscle soreness post-run. Focus on stretching major muscle groups such as your calves, hamstrings, quadriceps, and hip flexors. Hold each stretch for about 15-30 seconds, being careful not to push yourself to the point of pain.

Remember, warm-up and cool-down techniques are not time-consuming or complicated, but they are essential components of a successful running routine. By incorporating these techniques into your workouts, you will reduce the risk of injuries, improve your running performance, and enhance your overall enjoyment of jogging.

Jogging Your Way to a Healthier You

Establishing a regular exercise routine is crucial for maintaining good health, and people may choose various forms of exercise to achieve this goal. While jogging may not appeal to everyone, it proves to be a satisfying activity for some individuals.

In contrast to running, jogging involves a slower and more rhythmic pace, allowing for longer durations of activity compared to running. While some individuals can run at a slow pace, many often start running at a faster speed, slowing down or stopping when fatigue sets in, and then resuming a faster pace. Such a pattern can lead to quicker exhaustion and hinder the accomplishment of fitness goals.

Before starting your jogging routine, it's crucial to choose a safe and well-lit location with a level and smooth surface. Once you've identified a suitable area, you can start developing the jogging routine you aspire to follow. It's essential to start at a slow pace and gradually progress towards your desired level. If your goal is to jog for an hour daily, avoid attempting to start at that intensity; instead, begin gradually and incrementally to build up your endurance. Simultaneously, avoid the temptation to rush toward your goal within a week or two—listen to your body and allow it to guide you toward achieving your ultimate objective. There's no need to rush; reaching your fitness goal is a journey, and taking it easy is key, especially if you haven't incorporated jogging into your life until now.

As you work toward your ultimate goal, it's essential to maintain realistic expectations. Starting with a modest duration, like fifteen minutes, and gradually increasing it is a prudent approach. The objective is to achieve your final goal without subjecting yourself to excessive pain that hampers movement. Inducing pain through jogging is not a conducive way to develop an appreciation for this or any other physical activity. By commencing at a manageable pace that avoids significant discomfort, you're more likely to sustain your interest and commitment to jogging. Most individuals are reluctant to continue with an activity that consistently causes them pain. Incrementally extending the duration of your jogging sessions can significantly minimize this likelihood.

Chapter 3: Jogging and Walking

The Perfect Combination

If you find enjoyment in both jogging and walking or if jogging for extended periods is challenging, considering a blend of both activities might be beneficial. You can initiate your routine with jogging and, as fatigue or discomfort sets in, seamlessly transition to brisk walking. Many health professionals even assert that brisk walking offers superior benefits compared to running. Therefore, incorporating walking into your daily jog does not diminish the health advantages of jogging. In fact, combining the two activities can potentially increase your overall participation time, as opposed to attempting to exclusively jog or walk throughout the entire session.

A key reason why combining jogging with walking is advantageous lies in the distinct limitations each activity poses in terms of health benefits. Jogging excessively may lead to issues with knees and calves, while brisk walking might be too demanding for some individuals in a continuous session. By integrating both activities, you can manage the overall time spent, making it more accessible for those who find prolonged walking or jogging challenging.

However, the appropriateness of combining jogging with a leisurely walk depends on your goals for the jog. While a leisurely walk offers some benefits, they may not match those of a brisk walk. A leisurely walk might not sufficiently elevate your heart rate, especially for those following a weight loss plan. To attain the full benefits of aerobic exercises, maintaining a certain level of momentum and speed is essential. Adjusting your jog to a brisk walk is acceptable, but transforming it into a leisurely walk may not meet the required exercise intensity, particularly for those aligning their routine with a weight loss program.

Combining brisk walking with jogging can also serve as a preventive measure against certain issues associated with jogging. While not everyone encounters such problems, individuals with existing calf or knee issues can potentially reduce the risk of future complications through the strategic use of a combination of walking and jogging.

Optimizing Your Jogging Experience on a Track or Trail

When faced with the decision of where to jog, whether on a traditional jogging trail or a track, several factors come into play. A jogging trail may encompass diverse surfaces, ranging from park paths to neighborhood sidewalks, potentially featuring broken pavement, hard surfaces, and varying elevations. These conditions can pose challenges and even hidden hazards, leading to injuries.

On the other hand, a track typically consists of a softer surface, often dirt or another resilient material, contained within a defined area. The track provides a clear route with a known length, eliminating concerns about getting lost or being in unfamiliar and potentially unsafe areas after dark. However, not everyone has the convenience of proximity to a track, and public access to tracks, often situated in school or college athletic fields, may be restricted.

Before beginning a jogging regimen, it's advisable to decide whether a track or jogging trail aligns better with your preferences. Planning in advance allows you to identify suitable locations without wasting time searching when you're ready to start. If your jogging routine may require multiple locations, incorporate that into your pre-jogging research. Having several options lined up ensures a smoother transition into your jogging activity.

If uncertain about whether to opt for a track or trail, consider experimenting with both to gauge which one offers greater comfort. Taking the time for a "trial run" before establishing a routine allows you to gather essential information and determine which option suits you best. Preferences may vary, with some individuals favoring the softer track surface and others opting for the firmer terrain of a trail when embarking on their jogging routine.

Make Jogging a Group Activity

Often, when friends gather, they find themselves in search of new and engaging activities. Having exhausted familiar options, why not turn to jogging, walking, or running as a group endeavor? Bring your friends together and embark on a group jog through the neighborhood, a local park, or a nearby track. Not only does this offer a healthier alternative to routine outings, such as trips to the ice cream shop, but it also ensures enhanced safety in a larger group. While experts recommend at least two people for safety, being in the company of more individuals further enhances security. Making jogging a collective effort not only adds to the enjoyment but also promotes safety and simultaneous health benefits.

Whether you organize a group jog with friends or partake in a sponsored event, the key is participating in a group activity with peers. While the experience is likely more enjoyable with friends, don't discount the option of joining an organized activity if your friends aren't available. Don't deprive yourself of the opportunity to join a group jog or run simply because you're unfamiliar with the other participants. Such events provide an easy way to meet new people and forge new connections.

If you can't find a pre-existing sponsored event, there's no reason you can't initiate one yourself. All you need is a group of like-minded individuals interested in participating in a collective jogging, walking, or running activity. It can be organized like a game or simply involve providing healthy refreshments afterward. Organizing such an event doesn't demand excessive effort or time. Distribute flyers in your neighborhood to inform everyone about the gathering and gauge the level of interest. The more people interested, the more likely the event will be a success.

Participating in a group jogging, walking, or running effort isn't obligatory, but engaging with a community of friends or like-minded individuals can make the time more enjoyable, allowing you to accomplish your goals swiftly and efficiently. When you infuse an element of fun, time passes quickly, enabling you to surpass your initial goals effortlessly.

Chapter 4: Let Your Body Be Your Guide

A crucial aspect to bear in mind regarding jogging is to heed your body's signals and recognize when you've reached your limit. The duration of your jog, be it fifteen minutes or more, becomes secondary when discomfort arises in your calves and knees; it's imperative to cease the activity for the day. While you might believe that pushing through will have no lasting consequences, the reality is that failing to heed your body's warnings can lead to significant damage to your knees and calves. Even if you're an experienced jogger with years of experience, it's vital to halt when discomfort arises, as your body may be conveying important messages that should not be ignored.

A prevalent issue arises when individuals adhere to the mantra of "no pain, no gain." However, history has demonstrated that following this principle can result in more harm than good to the body. Continuing to exercise when one should have already ceased has led to irreversible damage to the legs and knees for many individuals. While it may seem like opting for the easier path, in truth, it involves safeguarding the body from potential further harm. Once muscles or cartilage are damaged, persistently exerting pressure on that tissue poses the risk of causing permanent and irreparable harm.

It's essential to recognize that jogging is not suitable for everyone, and, for some individuals, brisk walking proves to be the optimal form of exercise. If you've previously sustained knee injuries in other activities, it might be advisable to steer clear of jogging. The added stress on the knees could potentially exacerbate existing injuries. Prioritize safety and exercise caution not only during jogging but also in the selection of footwear for the activity. Never attempt jogging in regular street shoes or bare feet. Opt for sports shoes that provide the necessary support, preferably with cushioning, to avoid putting excessive pressure on the balls of your feet and risking damage.

Embracing your body's guidance is a principle that extends beyond the initiation of jogging; it's a practice that should accompany any exercise endeavor. Listening to your body becomes imperative, determining when it signals that you've reached your limit or when you possess the capacity to persist. The decisions you make in this regard will shape the scope of activities you can engage in throughout your lifetime. Therefore, considerations for your jogging routines should encompass a holistic perspective, recognizing that your body is a singular entity with interconnected components—muscles, bones, and cartilage—each deserving care and preservation. You only have one body, and safeguarding its internal elements is paramount.

Another common mistake individuals make is believing they must compensate for missed hours if they are sick, injured, or unable to participate in their usual jogging or running regimen. Engaging in such compensatory efforts places additional strain on the knees and calves and should be strictly avoided. This holds true not only for jogging but also for any aerobic or resistance exercise routine. Attempting to make up for lost exercise time is, in fact, one of the least beneficial actions you can take for your body.

Listening to your body is a crucial aspect of any jogging or running routine, ensuring that you engage in a healthy and sustainable exercise regimen. Your body provides valuable signals that can guide your training and help prevent injuries. Here are some key considerations for attentively tuning in to your body during your jogging or running sessions:

1. Awareness of Pain and Discomfort: Pay close attention to any pain or discomfort you may experience. While the discomfort associated with pushing your limits is normal, sharp or persistent pain could be indicative of an issue. If you encounter pain, it's essential to address it rather than push through, as it may lead to more severe injuries.

2. Monitoring Fatigue Levels: Understanding your fatigue levels is crucial for avoiding overtraining. If you find yourself consistently tired or lacking motivation, it might be a sign that your body needs rest. Incorporating rest days into your routine is as important as the active training days.

3. Adjusting Intensity and Pace: Your body's response to different intensities and paces can be a valuable guide. If you're feeling particularly energetic, you might push yourself a bit harder. Conversely, on days when your energy levels are lower, consider taking it easy with a slower pace or reduced intensity.

4. Hydration and Nutrition: Proper hydration and nutrition significantly impact your performance. Listen to signals of thirst and hunger, and ensure you're adequately fueled before, during, and after your run. Dehydration and inadequate nutrition can negatively affect your overall well-being and performance.

5. Recognizing Signs of Overtraining: Overtraining can lead to burnout and increased injury risk. Signs such as persistent fatigue, disrupted sleep, and changes in mood may indicate that your body needs more recovery time. It's crucial to strike a balance between pushing your limits and allowing sufficient recovery.

6. Adapting to Environmental Factors: Factors like weather conditions and terrain can influence how your body responds during a run. Adjust your pace and intensity based on these external factors to prevent pushing yourself too hard in challenging conditions.

7. Regular Self-Check: Conduct a self-check before, during, and after your run. Assess how your body feels overall, paying attention to specific areas like joints and muscles. This self-awareness can help you catch potential issues early on.

By actively listening to your body and responding to its signals, you'll not only enjoy a more fulfilling running experience but also promote long-term health and well-being. Remember that your body is your guide, and establishing a harmonious relationship with it is key to a sustainable and enjoyable jogging or running routine.

Chapter 5: Jogging, Running and Walking

The Aerobic Threesome

In the realm of aerobic exercise, jogging is just one component of a triad that includes running and walking. This combination forms a harmonious trio, each contributing to the vital benefits of aerobic exercise. Central to the significance of aerobic exercise is its ability to elevate the body's metabolism, facilitating calorie burning. This metabolic boost is instrumental in maintaining a healthy weight or accelerating the fat-burning process, surpassing caloric intake.

Jogging, running, and walking are three distinct yet interconnected forms of physical activity, each offering a range of health benefits and catering to diverse fitness levels. Here's a closer look at the unique attributes of jogging, running, and walking:

Walking is a low-impact, accessible, and beginner-friendly form of exercise that offers various health benefits. It is a natural and fundamental human movement, making it suitable for individuals of all fitness levels. Walking helps improve cardiovascular health, strengthen muscles, and maintain joint flexibility. It is an excellent option for those recovering from injuries, seniors, or individuals looking for a gentler form of exercise.

Jogging is a moderate-intensity aerobic exercise that falls between walking and running in terms of pace. It involves a gentle bounce or trot, usually at a pace faster than walking but slower than running. Jogging is an excellent cardiovascular workout that helps improve stamina, endurance, and overall cardiovascular health. It is often chosen by individuals seeking a middle-ground option that provides a more intense workout than walking without the impact associated with running.

Running is a higher-intensity form of aerobic exercise characterized by a faster pace and a more dynamic movement pattern than jogging. It involves a flight phase, where both feet are off the ground simultaneously. Running offers numerous health benefits, including improved cardiovascular fitness, enhanced muscular strength, and increased calorie burn. It is a popular choice for those looking to challenge themselves physically and engage in a more intense workout.

Benefits of Combined Activity

Incorporating a combination of jogging, running, and walking into a fitness routine can offer a well-rounded approach. This approach allows for flexibility, enabling individuals to tailor their workouts based on energy levels, fitness goals, and any physical limitations. Mixing these activities can provide variety, prevent monotony, and reduce the risk of overuse injuries.

Given that aerobic exercises serve as effective fat burners, the synergy of running, walking, and jogging emerges as an ideal combination. Engaging in all three activities throughout the day adds an element of ease and enjoyment, particularly if you incorporate brisk walking intermittently, avoiding the monotony associated with leisurely walking alone.

This trio of aerobic exercises ensures sustained enthusiasm, preventing fatigue or boredom from settling in during your exercise routine. Additionally, you have the flexibility to diversify your regimen by incorporating activities like skiing, bicycling, swimming, and HIIT circuit training, creating a comprehensive and enjoyable array of aerobic exercises.

Incorporating various exercises alongside jogging can achieve an optimal balance for boosting metabolism. Whether your goal is maintaining overall health or losing weight, understanding how to burn calories is crucial to prevent weight gain. The body needs to expend calories equal to its intake for weight maintenance or surpass the caloric intake to facilitate weight loss. This task can be challenging unless you engage in diverse exercises that aid in calorie burning. While jogging is often perceived as an enjoyable activity, it is essential to prioritize safety by wearing properly fitting shoes and choosing a secure exercise environment.

Combining jogging, running, and walking forms an effective amalgamation for those seeking weight maintenance or loss. Weight management doesn't necessarily require a strict diet but necessitates calorie burning, achievable through a diverse array of exercises. Jogging, with its rhythmic arm swings, enhances calorie expenditure, emphasizing the importance of sustained motivation and consistency.

Embracing the journey of your jogging or running routine entails navigating through both challenges and successes while infusing new elements to keep it enjoyable and dynamic, like walking. Sustaining a positive mindset and directing your focus toward the long-term benefits contribute to the overall well-being that running bestows.

Whether you choose to jog, run, or walk, the key is to engage in regular physical activity that aligns with your fitness goals and enhances your overall well-being. Each of these activities contributes to cardiovascular health, strengthens muscles, and supports mental wellness. The most important aspect is finding a balance that suits your individual needs and promotes a sustainable, enjoyable fitness routine. So, fasten your running shoes, step into the world, and savor the liberating experience that unfolds through the combination of jogging, walking, and running!

Chapter 6: Running 101 – The Basics

Understanding Different Types of Runs

In the world of running, the act of putting one foot in front of the other is merely the surface. To maximize your training and reach your running goals, a deeper understanding of the different types of runs is crucial. Each running session is designed with a distinct purpose, honing in on specific facets of your fitness and propelling your improvement as a runner. This section will explore the array of run types, providing you with a thorough insight into structuring your training regimen.

Easy Runs: Easy runs are the bread and butter of any running program, serving as fundamental components. Performed at a comfortable pace, these runs enable your body to recover and build endurance. They contribute to the improvement of cardiovascular fitness, facilitate fat burning, and foster the development of an efficient running form.

Long Runs: As implied by the name, long runs entail covering a greater distance compared to your standard training sessions. These runs play a vital role in fortifying both stamina and mental resilience. Additionally, long runs offer a chance to assess your endurance levels and refine your race-day fueling strategies.

Tempo Runs: Tempo runs involve maintaining a consistent and demanding pace, just below your lactate threshold. This type of run is instrumental in enhancing your lactate threshold, the point at which lactic acid starts accumulating in your muscles. Through training at this threshold, you can boost your body's capacity to efficiently eliminate lactic acid, ultimately allowing you to sustain a faster pace for extended durations.

Interval Training: Interval training involves cycling between high-intensity efforts and designated recovery intervals. This running technique proves highly effective in enhancing speed, power, and anaerobic fitness. By challenging your limits during intense intervals and strategically incorporating recovery periods, you can cultivate the capacity to maintain a swifter pace, particularly beneficial for race performance.

Hill Repeats: Ascending hills during your run poses a unique challenge to your muscles, increases power, and enhances running efficiency. The practice of hill repeats involves running up a hill with a sustained level of effort, followed by a period of jogging or walking downhill for recovery. Incorporating hill repeats into your training regimen also contributes to leg strengthening and fosters enhancements in your overall running form.

Fartlek Runs: Fartlek, a Swedish word meaning "speed play," involves alternating between bursts of fast running and slower recovery segments. Fartlek runs are flexible and unstructured, allowing you to vary the intensity and duration according to your preference. This type of run contributes to the enhancement of speed, endurance, and mental resilience.

Understanding the different types of runs will empower you to design a well-rounded training plan tailored to your goals. Remember to listen to your body, gradually increase the intensity and duration of each run, and always prioritize proper warm-up and cool-down routines. Happy running!

Designing a Weekly Training Schedule

One of the key elements in becoming a successful runner is establishing a well-structured and consistent training schedule. Whether you're a beginner or have been jogging for a while, having a weekly training plan can help you stay motivated, track your progress, and achieve your goals. In this subchapter, we will guide you through the process of designing a weekly training schedule that suits your fitness level and aspirations.

Once you understand your starting point, it's time to plan your weekly training schedule. A well-rounded plan should include a mix of different types of runs, rest days, and cross-training activities. Aim for at least three to four running days per week, allowing your body enough time to recover and adapt to the demands of running.

Beginners may want to start with a run-walk program, gradually increasing the running time and reducing walking intervals over several weeks. As you progress, incorporate easy-paced runs, tempo runs to improve your speed endurance, and long runs to build endurance. It's also important to include rest days to prevent overtraining and reduce the risk of injury. Use these days to recover, stretch, and focus on cross-training activities such as swimming or cycling to improve overall fitness.

Keep a training journal to track your progress and make necessary adjustments to your schedule. Monitor how your body responds to different types of workouts and gradually increase the intensity and duration as you feel comfortable. Remember, running should be enjoyable, so listen to your body and don't push yourself too hard too soon.

Preventing and Managing Running Injuries

Running is a fantastic way to stay fit, improve cardiovascular health, and boost overall well-being. However, it's important to be aware that injuries can occur if proper precautions are not taken. In this subchapter, we will discuss some essential tips and techniques for preventing and managing running injuries, ensuring that you can enjoy your jogging routine while minimizing the risk of harm.

1. Warm-up and Cool-down: Before every run, it's crucial to warm up your muscles with dynamic stretching exercises. This helps to increase blood flow, loosen up joints, and prepare your body for the upcoming workout. Similarly, after your run, performing static stretches during the cool-down phase helps prevent muscle stiffness and aids in recovery.

2. Gradual Progression: One common cause of running injuries is pushing yourself too hard, too soon. It's essential to gradually increase your running distance and intensity over time. This allows your body to adapt and become stronger, reducing the risk of overuse injuries.

3. Proper Footwear: Investing in good-quality running shoes that suit your foot type and running style is vital. Ill-fitting or worn-out shoes can lead to various injuries, including shin splints, plantar fasciitis, and stress fractures. Regularly replace your running shoes to maintain proper support and cushioning.

4. Cross-Training and Strength Training: Incorporating cross-training activities like swimming, cycling, or yoga into your routine can help prevent overuse injuries by giving your running muscles a break. Additionally, strength training exercises targeting your core, hips, and legs can improve stability and reduce the risk of injury.

5. Listen to Your Body: Pay attention to any pain, discomfort, or unusual sensations during or after running. Ignoring these warning signs can exacerbate existing injuries or lead to new ones. If you experience persistent pain, it's crucial to rest and seek medical advice to prevent further damage.

6. Injury Management: If you do sustain an injury, it's essential to take immediate action. RICE (Rest, Ice, Compression, Elevation) is the standard initial treatment for most running injuries. However, some injuries may require professional medical attention or physical therapy. Always consult a healthcare professional for an accurate diagnosis and appropriate treatment plan.

By following these preventive measures and adopting a sensible approach to training, you can greatly reduce the likelihood of running-related injuries. Remember, consistency and patience are key to a long and injury-free running journey. Happy and safe running!

Chapter 7: Getting Started with Running

Choosing the Right Running Shoes

When it comes to running, choosing the right shoes is critical for both comfort and injury prevention. With so many options available, it can be overwhelming to find the perfect pair. However, understanding the key factors to consider will help simplify the process and ensure you make the best choice for your running needs.

First and foremost, consider your foot type. There are three main types: neutral, overpronation, and underpronation. Neutral feet have a natural arch and roll slightly inward. Overpronators have low arches and tend to roll excessively inward, while underpronators have high arches and roll outward. Understanding your foot type will guide you towards shoes that provide the necessary support and cushioning.

Next, consider the terrain you will be running on. Road running shoes are designed for pavement and provide adequate cushioning and stability. Trail running shoes, on the other hand, are built to withstand uneven terrain and offer superior traction. If you plan on running on a mix of surfaces, consider versatile shoes that can handle both.

Another crucial factor to consider is shoe size and fit. Running shoes should provide a snug fit without being too tight or too loose. Your foot should not slide inside the shoe, and there should be enough room in the toe box to wiggle your toes comfortably. Remember, your feet may swell during longer runs, so it's essential to account for this when selecting the right size.

Furthermore, think about the level of cushioning and support you require. Cushioning is crucial for shock absorption, especially if you have joint issues or run long distances. Support features, such as medial posts or stability features, help control pronation and prevent overuse injuries. However, keep in mind that too much support can hinder natural foot movement, so finding the right balance is essential.

Lastly, consider your budget. While investing in a good pair of running shoes is important, it doesn't mean you have to break the bank. There are plenty of affordable options available that offer excellent quality and performance. Don't compromise on comfort and fit, but make sure to find a pair that suits your budget.

Remember, choosing the right running shoes is a personal decision. What works for one person may not work for another. It's essential to try on several options, jog around the store if possible, and seek advice from experts or experienced runners. By considering these key factors, you'll be one step closer to finding the perfect running shoes that will support your jogging journey and keep you running strong.

In conclusion, designing a weekly training schedule is essential for all runners, regardless of their experience level. By creating a balanced plan that includes a variety of workouts and rest days, you can improve your fitness, prevent injuries, and achieve your running goals. So lace up your shoes, grab a pen, and start planning your journey to becoming a better runner.

Tracking Progress and Adjusting Your Plan

As you embark on your journey to becoming a runner, it is essential to track your progress and make necessary adjustments along the way. This subchapter will guide you through the process of monitoring your development and fine-tuning your jogging plan to achieve the best possible results.

Tracking your progress can provide valuable insights into your running performance and help you stay motivated. One of the simplest ways to do this is by keeping a running log. In this log, you can record the distance you covered, the time it took, and any relevant notes about how you felt during the run. By consistently tracking this information, you can observe patterns, identify areas of improvement, and celebrate your achievements.

Another helpful tool in monitoring your progress is a fitness tracker or running app. These devices can provide valuable data such as your heart rate, pace, and calories burned. They also allow you to set goals and track your progress over time. By analyzing this data, you can identify areas where you need to push harder or areas where you may be overexerting yourself.

Once you have a clear understanding of your progress, it is crucial to adjust your jogging or running plan accordingly. This may involve increasing the distance or intensity of your runs gradually. However, it is essential to listen to your body and avoid pushing yourself too hard too soon, as this can lead to injuries or burnout.

Additionally, incorporating cross-training and strength exercises into your routine can enhance your overall performance and prevent injuries. Activities such as yoga, swimming, or cycling can help improve your flexibility, balance, and cardiovascular fitness. Strength exercises targeting your core, legs, and arms can also significantly benefit your running form and endurance.

Adjusting your plan also means being adaptable to external factors such as weather conditions or unexpected life events. If you are unable to follow your original schedule, be flexible and find alternative ways to stay active. Remember, consistency is key, and even small steps towards your goals are better than none at all.

In conclusion, tracking your progress and adjusting your plan are essential components of your running journey. By keeping a running log, using fitness trackers, and being adaptable, you can monitor your development, set new goals, and make the necessary adjustments to optimize your jogging experience. Stay committed, stay motivated, and enjoy the rewards of your hard work and dedication. Happy running!

Proper Running Form and Technique

In this subchapter, we will delve into the importance of proper running form and technique. Whether you are a seasoned runner or just starting out, understanding how to run with correct form can greatly enhance your running experience and help prevent injuries.

Running is a natural human movement, but it is crucial to maintain proper form to optimize efficiency and minimize strain on your body. The following tips will guide you towards developing a solid foundation for your running technique:

1. Posture: Maintain an upright posture while running. Keep your head up, eyes looking forward, and shoulders relaxed. Avoid slouching or leaning too far forward or backward, as this can lead to inefficient movement and increase the risk of injury.

2. Arm Swing: Your arms play a significant role in your running form. Keep your arms bent at a 90-degree angle and swing them naturally back and forth, not across your body. The movement of your arms should be coordinated with your legs, providing balance and momentum.

3. Footstrike: Aim for a midfoot or forefoot strike rather than a heel strike. Landing on your midfoot allows for a more efficient transfer of energy and reduces the impact on your joints. Avoid overstriding, which means landing with your foot too far in front of your body.

4. Cadence: Cadence refers to the number of steps you take per minute. Strive for a cadence of around 180 steps per minute, which promotes a quicker turnover and reduces the risk of overstriding. Count your steps for 30 seconds and multiply by two to calculate your cadence.

5. Breathing: Focus on deep, rhythmic breathing while running. Inhale deeply through your nose and exhale through your mouth. This helps deliver oxygen to your muscles efficiently and enhances endurance.

6. Core Engagement: Engage your core muscles by pulling your belly button in towards your spine. This stabilizes your torso and promotes a more efficient running form.

7. Relaxation: Strive for relaxation throughout your body while running. Tension in your muscles can lead to inefficient movement and wasted energy. Let go of any unnecessary tension and aim for a smooth, relaxed stride.

By incorporating these techniques into your running routine, you will not only improve your overall performance but also reduce the risk of common running injuries. Remember, practice makes perfect, so take the time to focus on your form and gradually make these adjustments a natural part of your running journey.

Whether you are a beginner or an experienced runner, mastering proper running form and technique is essential for maximizing your running potential and enjoying the sport to the fullest.

Building Endurance and Stamina

One of the keys to becoming a successful runner is building endurance and stamina. Whether you're just starting out or looking to improve your running performance, this subchapter will provide you with essential tips and techniques to help you go the distance.

Endurance is the ability to sustain physical activity over an extended period of time. By gradually increasing the duration and intensity of your runs, you can build your endurance and improve your cardiovascular fitness. Stamina, on the other hand, is the mental and physical strength to maintain a consistent pace throughout your run. Both endurance and stamina are crucial for runners of all levels.

To begin building endurance and stamina, it's important to start with a solid foundation. This means establishing a regular running routine and sticking to it. Consistency is key, so aim to run at least three to four times a week. Start with shorter distances and gradually increase the duration of your runs as your body adapts. Remember to listen to your body and take rest days when needed to avoid overtraining and injury.

In addition to regular running, incorporating cross-training exercises can also improve your endurance and stamina. Activities such as cycling, swimming, or strength training can help build overall fitness and prevent boredom from repetitive running. These exercises target different muscle groups and can enhance your running performance.

Incorporating Interval Training

Interval training is a highly effective method of enhancing your running performance, regardless of whether you are a beginner or an experienced runner. By alternating between high-intensity bursts of speed and recovery periods, interval training can help you improve your speed, endurance, and overall fitness level. In this subchapter, we will explore the benefits of interval training and provide you with some practical tips on how to incorporate it into your running routine.

One of the key advantages of interval training is its ability to maximize calorie burn in a shorter amount of time. By pushing your body to its limits during the high-intensity intervals, you can significantly increase your metabolic rate and continue to burn calories even after your workout has ended. This makes interval training an ideal choice for individuals who are looking to shed some extra pounds.

Another benefit of interval training is its ability to improve your cardiovascular fitness. By regularly challenging your heart and lungs with short bursts of intense effort, you can strengthen your cardiovascular system and improve your endurance. Over time, this will enable you to run faster and longer distances without feeling fatigued.

To incorporate interval training into your running routine, start by warming up with a gentle jog for about 5-10 minutes. Once you're warmed up, choose a landmark or set a timer to mark the beginning and end of each interval. Begin with a moderate intensity pace for your first interval, lasting about 1-2 minutes. Then, increase your speed to a challenging pace for the next 30-60 seconds. This should be a pace that feels uncomfortable but manageable. Repeat this cycle of high-intensity intervals followed by short recovery periods for a total of 10-15 minutes.

As a beginner, it's important to start with shorter intervals and gradually increase the duration and intensity as your fitness level improves. Aim to incorporate interval training into your running routine 1-2 times per week, allowing enough time for your body to recover between sessions. Remember to always listen to your body and adjust the intensity and duration of the intervals according to your comfort level.

If you would like to invest in a coaching program that can provide accountability and keep you consistent, check out Without Limits® of Wilmington, North Carolina. They provide training and coaching via a remote app and Training Peaks program and can work with you wherever you reside. Their coaching style is backed by science and shaped to fit your specific athletic goals, no matter how big or small. From endurance coaching to nutrition guidance to athletic events, they offer robust packages that are truly without limits. They truly believe that limits are self-imposed and can be overcome by changing our mentalities.

In conclusion, incorporating interval training into your running routine can yield remarkable results for runners of all levels. Whether you are looking to improve your speed, endurance, or overall fitness level, interval training can help you achieve your goals. By following the guidelines outlined in this subchapter, you can safely and effectively integrate this training method into your running regimen, taking your performance to new heights.

Chapter 8: Nutrition and Hydration for Runners

Fueling Your Body for Optimal Performance

Interval training is another effective method to boost endurance and stamina. By alternating between periods of intense effort and recovery, you can push your limits and increase your cardiovascular capacity. For example, try incorporating short bursts of faster running followed by a slower pace to recover. As you progress, you can gradually increase the duration and intensity of your intervals.

Proper nutrition and hydration are also important factors in building endurance and stamina. Fueling your body with a balanced diet, rich in carbohydrates, proteins, and healthy fats, will provide the energy needed for long runs. Hydrate adequately before, during, and after your runs to prevent dehydration and maintain optimal performance.

Lastly, don't forget the power of mental strength. Running long distances can be challenging, but developing a positive mindset and staying motivated will help you push through. Set realistic goals, celebrate your achievements, and find ways to enjoy your runs, whether it's through music, podcasts, or running with a friend.

By following these tips and techniques, you can gradually build your endurance and stamina, allowing you to run longer distances and achieve your running goals. Remember, consistency, patience, and perseverance are the keys to success in the world of running. So lace up your shoes, hit the pavement, and embrace the journey towards becoming a stronger, more resilient runner.

In order to achieve optimal performance during your running sessions, it is crucial to provide your body with the right fuel. Just like a car needs quality gasoline to run smoothly, your body requires proper nutrition to perform at its best. This subchapter will guide you through the essential aspects of fueling your body for running, helping you understand what to eat and when to eat it.

Before delving into the specifics, it is important to note that every individual is different, and what works for one person may not work for another. Therefore, it is essential to listen to your body and experiment with different strategies to determine what works best for you.

The foundation of fueling your body for running lies in a balanced and nutritious diet. Your meals should consist of a variety of whole foods, including lean proteins, complex carbohydrates, healthy fats, and an abundance of fruits and vegetables. These foods provide the necessary macronutrients and micronutrients your body needs to support your running endeavors.

Carbohydrates are particularly important for runners as they provide the primary source of energy. Aim to consume complex carbohydrates such as whole grains, legumes, and vegetables, as they release energy slowly and sustain you throughout your run. However, it is important to avoid consuming heavy meals close to your running sessions to prevent discomfort and digestive issues.

Hydration is another crucial aspect of fueling your body for optimal performance. Staying hydrated before, during, and after your runs is essential to maintain your energy levels and prevent dehydration. Make sure to drink water consistently throughout the day and consider electrolyte-replenishing beverages during longer runs or when running in hot weather.

Timing your meals and snacks appropriately is also key. Having a pre-run snack or meal about 1-2 hours before your run can provide you with the necessary energy boost. Experiment with different options such as a banana, a handful of nuts, or a small bowl of oatmeal to find what works best for you. Additionally, refueling your body with a post-run meal or snack containing a combination of carbohydrates and protein within 30-60 minutes after your run will aid in muscle recovery and replenishing glycogen stores.

Remember, fueling your body for optimal performance is not just about what you eat, but also about making sustainable lifestyle choices. Prioritize getting enough sleep, managing stress levels, and maintaining a consistent exercise routine to support your running journey.

By understanding the importance of fueling your body properly and making conscious choices about your nutrition, you will be able to enhance your running performance and reach new heights in your jogging journey.

Hydration Strategies for Runners

Staying properly hydrated is crucial for all runners, whether you are a beginner or an experienced athlete. As you engage in the invigorating activity of jogging, your body temperature rises, and you start to sweat, losing valuable fluids and electrolytes. In this subchapter, we will discuss essential hydration strategies to help you optimize your running performance and maintain your overall health.

First and foremost, it is important to hydrate before, during, and after your runs. Begin by drinking 16 to 20 ounces of water or a sports drink at least two hours before your run. This will ensure that your body is adequately hydrated before you even start jogging. During your run, aim to drink 4 to 8 ounces of fluid every 20 minutes to replenish what you lose through sweat. For longer runs, consider using a hydration pack or belt to carry water or sports drinks with you.

Choosing the right fluids is equally important. Water is an excellent choice for shorter runs under an hour, but for longer runs, you may want to supplement with sports drinks that contain electrolytes. These drinks help replace the sodium, potassium, and other minerals lost through sweat, aiding in maintaining a proper fluid balance in your body.

Another vital aspect of hydration for runners is post-run recovery. After completing your run, make it a habit to rehydrate within 30 minutes. Aim to drink 16 to 24 ounces of fluid, focusing on both water and sports drinks to replenish any lost electrolytes. Additionally, consuming a healthy snack or meal that includes a good mix of carbohydrates and proteins will aid in muscle recovery and replenishment.

It is essential to listen to your body's signals to determine if you are adequately hydrated. Signs of dehydration include dry mouth, dark-colored urine, fatigue, dizziness, and muscle cramps. If you experience any of these symptoms during or after your run, stop and rehydrate immediately.

Remember, hydration is a continuous process, not just limited to your running sessions. Make it a habit to drink water throughout the day, ensuring you are properly hydrated even on rest days. By following these hydration strategies, you will optimize your running performance, prevent dehydration-related complications, and enjoy a healthier and more enjoyable jogging experience.

In conclusion, proper hydration is a vital component of every runner's routine. By staying hydrated before, during, and after your runs, choosing the right fluids, and listening to your body's signals, you can ensure optimal performance and overall well-being. Make hydration a priority in your running journey, and you will reap the benefits of improved endurance, faster recovery, and a more enjoyable jogging experience.

Pre- and Post-Run Nutrition Tips

Proper nutrition is essential for any runner, whether you are a beginner or an experienced jogger. Fueling your body before and after a run can greatly enhance your performance, aid in recovery, and help you achieve your running goals. In this subchapter, we will explore some valuable pre- and post-run nutrition tips that every runner should know.

Pre-Run Nutrition Tips:

1. Hydration: Before heading out for a run, ensure you are adequately hydrated. Drink water or a sports drink at least 30 minutes before your run to maintain optimal fluid levels in your body.

2. Balanced Meals: Consume a balanced meal containing carbohydrates, proteins, and healthy fats approximately 2 to 3 hours before your run. This will provide you with sustained energy throughout your workout.

3. Quick Snacks: If you are short on time, opt for a light snack that is easily digestible. Examples include a banana, a handful of nuts, or a yogurt. These snacks will provide you with a quick burst of energy without weighing you down.

Post-Run Nutrition Tips:

1. Rehydrate: After a run, replenish lost fluids by drinking plenty of water. If you have been running for more than an hour or in hot weather, consider a sports drink to replace electrolytes.

2. Carbohydrates: Consume a post-run meal rich in carbohydrates to replenish glycogen stores in your muscles. This could include whole-grain bread, pasta, or fruits like berries or bananas.

3. Protein: Include protein in your post-run meal to aid in muscle recovery and repair. Opt for lean sources such as chicken, fish, eggs, or plant-based options like tofu or lentils.

4. Antioxidants: Incorporate foods rich in antioxidants to reduce inflammation caused by exercise. This includes colorful fruits and vegetables like berries, leafy greens, and bell peppers.

5. Timing is Key: Try to consume your post-run meal within 30 minutes to an hour after your workout. This is when your muscles are most receptive to nutrient absorption.

Remember, every runner is unique, and it may take some trial and error to find the nutrition routine that works best for you. Listen to your body, pay attention to how different foods make you feel, and make adjustments accordingly. By fueling your body with the right nutrients before and after your runs, you can optimize your performance and make the most out of your jogging journey.

Supplementation for Runners

In the world of running, there is a lot more to success than simply lacing up your shoes and hitting the pavement. While regular training, proper nutrition, and a well-designed running program are crucial, there is another aspect that can greatly enhance your performance and overall well-being as a runner: supplementation.

Supplements are not meant to replace a healthy diet, but they can provide additional support and fill in any nutritional gaps that may exist. Whether you are a beginner or a seasoned runner, incorporating certain supplements into your routine can help optimize your performance, aid in recovery, and support your overall health.

One of the most popular and widely studied supplements for runners is omega-3 fatty acids. These essential fats have been shown to reduce inflammation, improve cardiovascular health, and support joint function. They can be found in fish oil, flaxseed oil, and chia seeds.

Another key supplement for runners is vitamin D. Known as the "sunshine vitamin," vitamin D plays a crucial role in bone health, immune function, and muscle strength. Since runners often spend a lot of time outdoors, it's important to ensure adequate vitamin D levels. However, depending on your location and the time of year, it may be challenging to get enough sunlight exposure. In such cases, vitamin D supplements can be beneficial.

Creatine is a supplement that can aid in increasing muscle strength and power. It works by providing additional energy to the muscles during high-intensity activities, such as sprints or hill repeats. While creatine is more commonly associated with weightlifting, it can benefit runners by improving their overall speed and power output.

Lastly, probiotics are essential for gut health, which plays a significant role in the overall well-being of runners. Regular running can put stress on the digestive system, leading to issues such as bloating, cramping, or an upset stomach. Probiotics help maintain a healthy balance of gut bacteria, improving digestion, and reducing gastrointestinal distress.

Before incorporating any supplements into your routine, it's important to consult with a healthcare professional or a registered dietitian. They can assess your individual needs and provide personalized recommendations based on your goals and current health status.

Remember, supplements are meant to complement a healthy lifestyle, not replace it. They should be used in conjunction with proper nutrition, regular exercise, and adequate rest. By incorporating the right supplements into your routine, you can optimize your running performance and support your overall well-being as a runner.

Runners Essentials Daily Vitamin Formula is a groundbreaking nutritional supplement, specifically targeted for runners and endurance athletes. The Proprietary Blend is uniquely formulated for the nutritional needs of runners. Learn more about this vitamin for runners at Runners Essentials.

Chapter 9: Mental Strength and Motivation

Developing a Positive Mindset for Running

In the world of running, physical fitness is just one piece of the puzzle. Equally important, if not more so, is developing a positive mindset. Whether you are a beginner or an experienced runner, cultivating a positive mindset will not only enhance your running experience but also help you overcome obstacles and achieve your goals. In this subchapter, we will explore strategies and techniques to develop a positive mindset for running.

First and foremost, it is essential to set realistic and achievable goals. When starting your running journey, it is easy to get caught up in comparing yourself to others or setting unrealistic expectations. Instead, focus on personal growth and progress. Set small milestones along the way, such as running for a specific distance or improving your pace, and celebrate each achievement. By setting realistic goals, you will build confidence and motivation, leading to a more positive mindset.

Another crucial aspect of developing a positive mindset is cultivating self-belief. Believe in your abilities and trust the process. Remind yourself of your past accomplishments and how far you have come. Positive self-talk can be a powerful tool. Replace self-doubt and negative thoughts with positive affirmations. Repeat phrases such as "I am strong," "I can do this," and "I am becoming a better runner every day." Over time, these positive affirmations will become ingrained in your mindset, boosting your confidence and resilience.

Staying motivated is an ongoing challenge for runners of all levels. To maintain motivation, find what inspires you. Whether it is listening to uplifting music, reading motivational quotes, or visualizing your goals, find techniques that resonate with you. Surround yourself with a supportive community of fellow runners who can provide encouragement and share experiences. Remember, running is not just a physical activity; it is a mental and emotional journey as well.

Lastly, embrace the joys of running. Focus on the present moment, the feeling of your feet hitting the pavement, the rhythm of your breath, and the sights and sounds around you. Running can be a form of meditation that allows you to clear your mind and find inner peace. By embracing the beauty of the present moment, you will develop a positive mindset and enjoy the journey of running.

In conclusion, developing a positive mindset is crucial for runners of all levels. By setting realistic goals, cultivating self-belief, staying motivated, and embracing the joys of running, you will enhance your running experience and achieve your full potential. Remember, running is not just about physical fitness; it is a holistic journey that requires a positive mindset. So lace up your running shoes, embrace the challenge, and let your positive mindset propel you forward on your running journey.

Overcoming Mental Barriers and Challenges

In the journey of becoming a runner, many beginners face not only physical challenges but also mental barriers that can hinder their progress. Running is not just about the physical act of putting one foot in front of the other; it requires mental strength and resilience. In this subchapter, we will explore some common mental barriers and challenges that beginners may encounter and provide strategies to overcome them.

One of the most common mental barriers in running is the fear of failure. Many beginners doubt their abilities and worry about not being able to complete a run or meet their goals. It is important to remember that everyone starts somewhere, and progress takes time. Setting realistic goals and focusing on gradual improvements can help overcome this fear. Celebrate small victories and acknowledge the progress made along the way.

Another mental challenge is the lack of motivation. It is natural to feel demotivated at times, especially when faced with obstacles or plateaus. To overcome this, it is essential to find your personal motivation. Whether it is improving your health, relieving stress, or achieving a fitness milestone, identifying your motivation can help you stay focused and committed. Surrounding yourself with a supportive community or joining a running group can also provide the necessary encouragement and accountability.

Negative self-talk is another mental barrier that can hinder progress. It is easy to fall into a pattern of self-doubt and criticism. However, practicing positive affirmations and reframing negative thoughts can help shift your mindset towards a more positive outlook. Replace thoughts like "I can't do this" with "I am capable of improving every day." Developing a growth mindset and believing in your potential is crucial for overcoming mental barriers.

Lastly, it is important to manage stress and anxiety. Running can be an excellent way to alleviate stress, but it can also become a source of anxiety. Learning relaxation techniques, such as deep breathing or visualization, can help calm the mind before and during a run. Additionally, incorporating mindfulness practices into your training routine can help you stay present and focused on the present moment.

In conclusion, overcoming mental barriers and challenges is an integral part of the running journey. By acknowledging and addressing these barriers, beginners can develop the mental resilience necessary to achieve their goals. Remember that running is not just a physical activity; it is a mental and emotional journey of self-discovery and growth. Embrace the challenges, celebrate the victories, and keep pushing forward. You are capable of more than you think.

Setting Realistic Expectations

When it comes to starting a new running routine, it is essential to set realistic expectations for yourself. Many beginners often fall into the trap of expecting immediate results or pushing themselves too hard, leading to frustration and even injuries. In this subchapter, we will discuss the importance of setting realistic expectations and how it can help you achieve long-term success in your running journey.

First and foremost, it is crucial to understand that running is a gradual process. Rome wasn't built in a day, and the same applies to your running abilities. It takes time for your body to adapt and become accustomed to the demands of running. While it is natural to want to progress quickly, setting unrealistic goals can lead to disappointment and demotivation. Instead, focus on small, attainable milestones that will help you build a strong foundation and gradually improve your running performance.

Additionally, it is essential to listen to your body and acknowledge its limits. Pushing yourself too hard or ignoring signs of fatigue can result in injuries that may set you back significantly. Remember, running should be enjoyable and sustainable in the long run. Set a pace that feels comfortable for you and gradually increase your intensity and distance as your body becomes stronger and more conditioned.

Another aspect of setting realistic expectations is understanding that progress is not always linear. Some days, you may feel like you're on top of the world, while other days may feel more challenging. It's crucial to accept these fluctuations and not let them discourage you. Remember that even the most experienced runners have their off days. Stay positive, trust the process, and celebrate even the smallest victories along the way.

Finally, it is important to note that everyone's running journey is unique. Comparing yourself to others or expecting to achieve the same results as someone else can be counterproductive. Focus on your own progress and celebrate your personal achievements. Remember that running is a personal journey that should be tailored to your own abilities and goals.

In conclusion, setting realistic expectations is vital for any beginner runner. By understanding that progress takes time, listening to your body, accepting fluctuations, and embracing your individual journey, you will set yourself up for long-term success in your running endeavors. So lace up your shoes, take it one step at a time, and enjoy the journey of becoming a runner!

Staying Motivated and Consistent with Your Running Routine

Consistency is the key to success in any endeavor, and running is no exception. Whether you are a beginner or have been jogging for a while, it can be challenging to stay motivated and stick to your running routine. In this subchapter, we will explore some tips and strategies to help you maintain your motivation and consistency while embarking on your running journey.

1. Set Clear and Realistic Goals: Start by setting clear and achievable goals for yourself. These goals could be anything from completing a 5K race to running for 30 minutes without stopping. Having a specific target to work towards will keep you focused and motivated.

2. Find Your Why: Understanding why you want to run can be a powerful motivator. Whether it is to improve your fitness, lose weight, reduce stress, or simply enjoy the outdoors, identifying your underlying reasons will help you stay committed, especially on days when you feel less motivated.

3. Create a Schedule: Establish a regular running schedule that fits into your daily routine. Decide on the days and times that you will dedicate to running and treat them as non-negotiable appointments with yourself. Consistency breeds habit, and soon enough, running will become an integral part of your life.

4. Mix It Up: Variety is the spice of life, and it applies to running too. Try different routes, terrains, and distances to keep your runs interesting. Experiment with interval training, hill runs, or even incorporating other forms of exercise like strength training or yoga. This variety will prevent boredom and help you stay engaged with your running routine.

5. Join a Running Group or Find a Running Buddy: Running with others can provide a tremendous boost to your motivation. Join a local running group or find a running buddy who shares your goals. Having someone to hold you accountable and share the joys and challenges of running can make the entire experience more enjoyable and rewarding.

6. Track Your Progress: Keep a record of your runs, including distance, time, and any notes about how you felt during the run. Seeing your progress over time will give you a sense of accomplishment and motivate you to keep going.

7. Celebrate Milestones: Celebrate your achievements along the way. Whether it's completing your first mile, reaching a new personal best, or conquering a race, take the time to acknowledge and reward yourself for your hard work and dedication.

In conclusion, maintaining motivation and consistency in your running routine is a journey that brings both challenges and rewards. Embracing the ups and downs, staying positive, and focusing on the long-term benefits that running brings to your physical and mental well-being are essential. Your running journey is not just about the miles you cover but the resilience you build, the goals you achieve, and the overall sense of well-being you attain. So, lace up your running shoes, step into the world, and enjoy the freedom, vitality, and satisfaction that a dedicated running routine can bring to your life. Happy running!

Chapter 10: Running for Weight Loss and Fitness

Incorporating Running into a Weight Loss Plan

If you're looking to shed some extra pounds and improve your overall fitness, incorporating running into your weight loss plan can be a game-changer. Running is a fantastic cardiovascular exercise that helps burn calories and boost your metabolism, making it an effective tool for achieving your weight loss goals. In this subchapter, we will explore how to seamlessly integrate running into your weight loss plan, ensuring optimal results and a sustainable approach.

Before embarking on your running journey, it's essential to set realistic goals. Start by evaluating your current fitness level and determining how much time you can dedicate to running each week. Remember, consistency is key, so it's better to start with shorter, more frequent runs rather than sporadic long sessions.

To make running a more enjoyable experience, invest in a good pair of running shoes that provide adequate support and cushioning. Ill-fitting shoes can lead to discomfort and potential injuries, hindering your progress. Additionally, wear comfortable clothing that allows for freedom of movement and wicks away sweat, keeping you cool and dry.

One of the most effective ways of incorporating running into your weight loss plan is by following a structured training program. These programs gradually increase your running distance and intensity, allowing your body to adapt and avoid overexertion. Whether you're a complete beginner or have some running experience, there are various training plans available, such as Couch to 5K or interval training, catering to different fitness levels.

Diet plays a crucial role in any weight loss plan, and running is no exception. While running can help create a calorie deficit, it's important to fuel your body with nutritious foods to support your overall health and performance. Incorporate a balanced diet rich in fruits, vegetables, whole grains, and lean proteins. Stay hydrated by drinking plenty of water before, during, and after your runs.

To stay motivated on your weight loss journey, consider joining a running group or finding a running buddy. Having a support system can provide accountability and make running more enjoyable. Additionally, track your progress by using a running app or a fitness tracker to monitor your distance, pace, and calories burned.

Remember, running is a lifelong journey, and weight loss takes time. Be patient with yourself and celebrate small victories along the way. By incorporating running into your weight loss plan, you're not only working towards shedding those extra pounds but also improving your cardiovascular health and overall well-being. So lace up those running shoes and get ready to embrace the transformative power of running!

Maximizing Calorie Burn During Your Runs

Running is not only a great way to improve your cardiovascular fitness and endurance, but it is also an excellent activity for burning calories and shedding unwanted pounds. By incorporating a few simple strategies into your running routine, you can maximize your calorie burn and get the most out of your workouts. Whether you are a beginner or have been running for a while, these tips will help you take your calorie-burning potential to the next level.

First and foremost, it's important to establish a consistent running routine. Aim for at least three to four runs per week, gradually increasing your distance and intensity as your fitness level improves. Consistency is key when it comes to burning calories, as regular running sessions help elevate your metabolism and keep it elevated throughout the day.

To further amplify your calorie burn, consider incorporating interval training into your runs. Interval training involves alternating between periods of high-intensity running and low-intensity recovery periods. This method is incredibly effective at boosting your metabolism and increasing overall calorie expenditure. Start by incorporating short bursts of high-intensity running, gradually increasing the duration and intensity over time. Not only will this help you burn more calories during your run, but it will also elevate your metabolism for hours after your workout.

Another effective strategy for maximizing calorie burn is to vary the terrains and inclines of your runs. Running on different surfaces, such as trails or hills, engages different muscles and increases the intensity of your workout. Uphill running, in particular, requires more effort and burns a greater number of calories compared to running on flat surfaces. Incorporating hills or inclines into your runs can help you burn more calories and build strength in your legs.

In addition to varying your terrains, consider adding resistance training exercises to your running routine. Strength training helps build lean muscle mass, which in turn increases your metabolism and calorie burn even when you're at rest. By incorporating exercises such as squats, lunges, and planks into your routine, you will not only improve your running performance but also increase your overall calorie burn.

Lastly, don't forget about the importance of proper nutrition and hydration. Fueling your body with the right nutrients before and after your runs helps optimize your calorie burn and aids in muscle recovery. Stay hydrated throughout your runs by drinking water or sports drinks, especially on hot and humid days. Proper nutrition and hydration are crucial for sustaining energy levels and maximizing calorie burn during your runs.

By implementing these strategies into your running routine, you can maximize your calorie burn and make the most of your workouts. Remember to start gradually and listen to your body to avoid injuries. Running is a fantastic way to not only improve your fitness but also burn calories and achieve your weight loss goals. Lace up your running shoes, hit the pavement, and watch the calories melt away!

Strength Training for Runners

In the world of running, it is often easy to focus solely on the miles logged and the speed achieved. However, incorporating strength training into your routine can greatly enhance your performance, prevent injuries, and take your running to the next level. This subchapter will explore the importance of strength training for runners and provide practical tips on how to incorporate it into your training regimen.

Strength training is a vital component of overall fitness for any athlete, including runners. It not only helps build muscle strength but also improves balance, stability, and joint mobility. By strengthening your muscles, tendons, and ligaments, you can better withstand the repetitive impact and stress that running puts on your body.

One of the key benefits of strength training for runners is injury prevention. By strengthening the muscles that support your joints, such as the hips, glutes, and core, you can reduce the risk of common running injuries such as IT band syndrome, shin splints, and knee pain. Additionally, a stronger body can improve your running form, leading to better efficiency and reduced fatigue.

When it comes to strength training exercises for runners, a combination of bodyweight exercises, resistance training, and flexibility exercises is recommended. Bodyweight exercises such as squats, lunges, and planks are great for building leg and core strength. Resistance training with weights or resistance bands can target specific muscle groups, such as the calves, quads, and hamstrings. It is also important to incorporate flexibility exercises, such as yoga or dynamic stretches, to improve your range of motion and prevent muscle imbalances.

To incorporate strength training into your running routine, aim for two to three sessions per week. Start with lighter weights and gradually increase the intensity as your strength improves. It is essential to allow for proper rest and recovery between strength training sessions to avoid overtraining and fatigue.

Remember, strength training should be viewed as a complement to your running, not a replacement. Be sure to continue your regular running workouts while incorporating strength training into your routine. As your strength increases, you may notice improvements in your running performance, endurance, and overall fitness.

In conclusion, strength training is a valuable addition to any runner's training regimen. By incorporating strength exercises into your routine, you can improve your running performance, prevent injuries, and enhance your overall fitness. So, lace up your running shoes and get ready to take your running to new heights with the power of strength training.

Cross-Training Options for Overall Fitness

In the pursuit of overall fitness, cross-training can be an excellent addition to your running routine. By incorporating different activities into your fitness regimen, you can improve your cardiovascular endurance, strengthen different muscle groups, prevent injuries, and enhance your overall performance. In this subchapter, we will explore various cross-training options that complement running and contribute to your overall fitness.

One of the most popular cross-training activities is cycling. Whether you prefer outdoor cycling or using a stationary bike, this low-impact exercise can be a fantastic way to enhance your cardiovascular endurance without putting excessive strain on your joints. Cycling also targets different leg muscles, such as the quadriceps, hamstrings, and calves, which can help improve your running performance and prevent muscle imbalances.

Another effective cross-training option is swimming. Swimming is a full-body workout that engages multiple muscle groups simultaneously. It provides an excellent opportunity for low-impact cardiovascular exercise, while also improving flexibility, endurance, and core strength. Additionally, swimming can act as a form of active recovery, allowing your body to heal and rejuvenate after intense running sessions.

If you prefer activities that focus on strength and flexibility, consider incorporating yoga or Pilates into your routine. Both these practices can help improve your posture, balance, and flexibility, which are crucial for efficient running mechanics. Yoga also provides mental benefits such as stress reduction and improved focus, which can positively impact your running performance.

High-intensity interval training (HIIT) is another cross-training option worth exploring. HIIT workouts involve short bursts of intense exercise followed by brief recovery periods. These workouts can be done using bodyweight exercises, kettlebells, or other equipment, and they effectively improve cardiovascular fitness, build strength, and burn calories. HIIT sessions can be tailored to suit all fitness levels and can be a great way to improve your speed and power as a runner.

When incorporating HIIT into your running training, start gradually and consider the following:

Frequency: Begin with one to two sessions per week and assess how your body responds.

Intensity: Tailor the intensity to your fitness level, gradually increasing it as you build strength and endurance.

Rest and Recovery: Allow adequate time for recovery between HIIT sessions to prevent overtraining and reduce the risk of injury.

Balance with Running: HIIT should complement, not replace, your running routine. Integrate it strategically, perhaps on days when you're not doing intense running workouts.

Always consult with a fitness professional or healthcare provider before starting a new training program, especially if you have pre-existing health conditions or concerns.

In conclusion, cross-training is a valuable addition to any running program, regardless of your fitness level or goals. Cycling, swimming, yoga, Pilates, and HIIT are just a few examples of cross-training activities that can improve your overall fitness, prevent injuries, and enhance your running performance. By incorporating these options into your routine, you'll not only become a stronger runner but also enjoy the variety and benefits that come with a well-rounded fitness regimen.

Chapter 11: Participating in Races and Events

Choosing the Right Race for Your Goals

When it comes to running, setting goals is an integral part of the journey. Whether you are a beginner or an experienced runner, having a race to work towards can provide the motivation and focus you need to stay committed. However, with countless races available, how do you choose the right one for your goals? This subchapter will guide you through the process of selecting the perfect race that aligns with your aspirations and abilities.

First and foremost, it is crucial to understand your current fitness level and running capabilities. If you are new to running, it might be wise to start with a shorter distance race, such as a 5K or 10K. These races are beginner-friendly and offer a great opportunity to build your endurance and confidence. On the other hand, if you have been running for a while and are looking to challenge yourself, consider signing up for a half-marathon or even a full marathon.

Next, consider your personal goals. Are you running to improve your overall fitness, lose weight, or compete for a personal record? Different races cater to various objectives. For instance, if you are interested in improving your speed, you may want to look for races that offer a flat and fast course. Alternatively, if you are seeking a more scenic and enjoyable experience, trail races might be the perfect fit for you.

Another important factor to consider is the time commitment required for training. Some races demand more extensive training schedules, while others are more forgiving. Be honest with yourself about the amount of time you can dedicate to training, as this will greatly impact your race selection.

Additionally, take into account logistical aspects such as the race location, date, and cost. If you prefer to run in your local area, search for races that are nearby. Consider your schedule and availability when choosing the race date. Moreover, evaluate the registration fees and any additional costs associated with the race, such as travel expenses or accommodation.

Finally, do thorough research on the races you are considering. Read reviews from previous participants, check the race's reputation, and examine the course map. This will give you a better understanding of what to expect and help you make an informed decision.

Remember, the right race for your goals should challenge and excite you. It should push you out of your comfort zone while still being achievable. By taking into account your fitness level, personal objectives, time commitment, logistics, and conducting thorough research, you can confidently choose a race that aligns with your goals and sets you on a path to success.

Training for a 5K, 10K, Half Marathon, or Marathon

Whether you are a beginner looking to challenge yourself or an experienced runner aiming to improve your performance, training for a 5K, 10K, half marathon, or marathon requires dedication, commitment, and a well-structured plan. In this subchapter, we will guide you through the essential elements of training for these races, providing you with the knowledge and tools necessary to achieve your running goals.

Firstly, it's important to establish a strong foundation before embarking on any race-specific training. This involves gradually increasing your weekly mileage and incorporating regular runs into your routine. By building endurance through consistent running, you will prepare your body for the challenges of longer distances.

Next, it's crucial to incorporate a variety of training methods into your schedule. This includes both easy runs for recovery and longer runs to build endurance. Speed workouts, such as intervals or tempo runs, will help improve your pace and build strength. Additionally, cross-training activities like cycling or swimming can complement your running and reduce the risk of injury.

To optimize your training, it's important to listen to your body and avoid overtraining. Rest and recovery days are just as important as your training days. They allow your muscles to repair and adapt, leading to improved performance. Also, don't forget to incorporate strength training exercises to build muscle, prevent injury, and improve running economy.

In addition to physical training, nutrition plays a vital role in maximizing your performance. Fueling your body with a balanced diet, rich in carbohydrates, protein, and healthy fats, will provide you with the energy needed to perform at your best. Adequate hydration before, during, and after your runs is also crucial to maintain optimal performance and prevent dehydration.

Finally, mental preparation is key to overcoming the challenges of long-distance running. Developing a positive mindset, setting realistic goals, and visualizing success can significantly impact your performance. Surrounding yourself with a supportive community of fellow runners or joining a running group can provide motivation and encouragement throughout your training journey.

Remember, training for a 5K, 10K, half marathon, or marathon is a personal journey, and each individual's progress will vary. Embrace your own pace and enjoy the process. With patience, dedication, and a well-structured training plan, you'll be well on your way to crossing the finish line and achieving your running goals.

Training for races like a 5K, 10K, half marathon, or marathon involves strategic planning, progressive workouts, and a commitment to consistent training. Here's a guide tailored to each distance:

Training for a 5K:

Build a Running Foundation:

Start with a mix of walking and jogging if you're new to running. Gradually increase running intervals and reduce walking time. Aim for 3-4 workouts per week, including both running and rest days.

Interval Training:

Introduce interval training to improve speed and endurance. Include workouts like sprinting for 30 seconds followed by a 1-minute recovery jog.

Longer Runs:

Slowly extend your running distance. Aim for one longer run per week to build stamina.

Strength and Flexibility:

Include strength training exercises for overall fitness. Incorporate dynamic stretches to improve flexibility.

Rest and Recovery:

Prioritize rest days to prevent burnout and reduce the risk of injury. Listen to your body and adjust training intensity accordingly.

Training for a 10K:

Base Building:

Ensure you can comfortably run 5K before starting 10K training. Gradually increase weekly mileage with a mix of short and long runs.

Interval and Tempo Runs:

Integrate intervals and tempo runs to improve speed and endurance. Include hill training for added strength.

Long Runs:

Extend your long runs progressively, aiming for distances beyond 6 miles. Focus on a consistent pace during these longer runs.

Cross-Training:

Incorporate cross-training activities like cycling or swimming. Strengthen core muscles to improve overall stability.

Training for a Half Marathon:

Consistent Running:

Have a solid running base, ideally having completed a 10K. Incorporate 3-4 running days per week.

Progressive Long Runs:

Gradually increase the distance of your long runs, peaking around 10-12 miles. Include a step-back week for recovery every 3-4 weeks.

Pace and Race Simulation:

Practice your goal race pace during training runs. Include a couple of race simulation workouts to prepare mentally.

Nutrition and Hydration:

Pay attention to fueling strategies during long runs. Experiment with nutrition and hydration plans that work for you.

Training for a Full Marathon:

Marathon-Ready Base:

Build a solid running foundation with experience in half marathons. Ensure you're injury-free before starting marathon training.

Higher Mileage:

Gradually increase weekly mileage, with a peak of around 20-22 miles. Include regular long runs, building up to 18-22 miles.

Back-to-Back Long Runs:

Integrate back-to-back long runs to simulate marathon fatigue. Consider "tune-up" races to practice pacing and race-day logistics.

Tapering:

Allow for a proper tapering period before the marathon. Reduce mileage but maintain intensity to arrive at the race feeling fresh.

Mental Toughness:

Practice mental strategies to cope with the challenges of a marathon. Develop a race-day plan, including pacing and fueling strategies.

Always tailor your training plan to your fitness level, listen to your body, and consider consulting with a running coach or healthcare professional, especially if you have specific health concerns or goals.

These are some invaluable tips from *Without Limits® Coaching* to enhance your racing experience. While these guidelines offer general advice, be sure to stick to any personalized plans you've discussed with your coach.

Race Day Preparation and Strategies

Preparing for race day is crucial for runners of all levels. Whether you are a beginner or have been jogging for a while, having a solid race day plan can make a significant difference in your performance. In this subchapter, we will discuss various race day preparation tips and strategies that will help you achieve your running goals.

Firstly, it is important to have a clear understanding of the race course. Familiarize yourself with the route, including any challenging hills or turns. This knowledge will allow you to plan your pace and conserve energy accordingly. Additionally, knowing the location of water stations and restrooms along the course will help you stay hydrated and comfortable throughout the race.

Next, consider your nutrition and hydration leading up to race day. It is essential to fuel your body with the right nutrients to ensure optimal performance on race day. Consume a balanced diet consisting of lean proteins, complex carbohydrates, and healthy fats. Avoid trying new foods before the race, as it may upset your stomach. Hydration is equally important, so remember to drink plenty of water in the days leading up to the race.

Another crucial aspect of race day preparation is mental readiness. Visualize yourself crossing the finish line and achieving your goals. Develop positive affirmations and repeat them to yourself during the race. Additionally, practice relaxation techniques, such as deep breathing or meditation, to calm your nerves before the race starts.

On race day, arrive early to avoid any last-minute stress. This will give you ample time to warm up, stretch, and get mentally prepared. Dress appropriately for the weather conditions and wear comfortable running shoes that have been broken in. Consider wearing a race bib and use safety pins to secure it to your shirt.

During the race, strategize your pace based on your training and fitness level. Start at a comfortable pace and gradually increase your speed as you progress through the course. Don't be afraid to take walking breaks if needed, especially during longer races. Remember to listen to your body and adjust your strategy accordingly.

These are some invaluable tips from *Without Limits® Coaching* to enhance your racing experience. While these guidelines offer general advice, be sure to stick to any personalized plans you've discussed with your coach.

In conclusion, race day preparation and strategies are essential for runners of all levels. By familiarizing yourself with the race course, fueling your body properly, and mentally preparing yourself, you can optimize your performance. Arriving early, dressing appropriately, and strategizing your pace will further contribute to a successful race day. Remember to enjoy the experience and celebrate your achievements, regardless of the outcome. Happy running!

Post-Race Recovery and Celebration

Congratulations! You've just crossed the finish line of your first race. It's an incredible achievement, and now it's time to focus on post-race recovery and celebration. In this subchapter, we will explore the essential steps you should take to recover properly and acknowledge your accomplishment.

Recovery plays an integral role in your running journey. It allows your body to heal and repair the muscles that have worked so hard during the race. Firstly, make sure to cool down by walking or slow jogging for 5-10 minutes. This will help your heart rate return to normal and prevent any sudden dizziness or fainting. Stretching your muscles afterwards can also help alleviate soreness and prevent stiffness.

Hydration is key after a race, as your body has lost a significant amount of fluids through sweat. Drink plenty of water or sports drinks to replenish electrolytes and prevent dehydration. It's also important to refuel your body with nutritious food, focusing on a combination of carbohydrates and protein. This will aid in muscle recovery and replenish energy stores.

Rest and sleep are essential components of the recovery process. Your body needs time to recover and rebuild. Listen to your body and allow yourself to rest for a day or two after the race. This will help prevent injuries and ensure you're ready to return to your running routine.

While recovery is crucial, it's equally important to celebrate your achievement. Take a moment to reflect on all the hard work and dedication you put into training for this race. Treat yourself to a special meal or indulge in a small reward. Share your accomplishment with friends and family who have supported you throughout your journey. Celebrating your success will boost your confidence and motivate you for future races.

Finally, don't forget to evaluate your race performance. Reflect on what went well and what you could improve for future races. This self-assessment will help you set new goals and continue progressing as a runner.

In conclusion, post-race recovery and celebration are vital aspects of your running journey. By following these essential steps, you'll ensure a smooth recovery and acknowledge your accomplishments. Remember to relax, refuel, and reflect before embarking on new running adventures. Run happy!

Chapter 12: Road Safety and Etiquette

Safety Tips for Running Outdoors

Running outdoors is a fantastic way to stay fit and enjoy the beauty of nature. Whether you are a beginner or an experienced runner, it is crucial to prioritize your safety while hitting the pavement. This subchapter aims to equip you with essential safety tips for running outdoors, ensuring a secure and enjoyable running experience.

1. Choose well-lit areas: When running outdoors, opt for well-lit routes, especially during early mornings or late evenings. This not only helps you stay visible to others but also minimizes the risk of accidents and potential hazards.

2. Wear reflective gear: To enhance your visibility, wear reflective clothing, such as vests, armbands, or shoes with reflective strips. This is crucial when running in low-light conditions or along busy roads.

3. Stay alert and aware: Always be mindful of your surroundings while running outdoors. Keep an eye out for vehicles, cyclists, pedestrians, and potential hazards like potholes or uneven pavements. Avoid distractions, such as using headphones at a high volume, to ensure you can hear approaching vehicles or other potential dangers.

4. Adhere to traffic regulations: Approach running with the same considerations as any other road user. Utilize the sidewalk when accessible, and if running on the road is necessary, face oncoming traffic. Respect traffic signals and employ designated crosswalks when navigating road crossings.

5. Inform someone about your route: Before heading out for a run, let someone know your planned route and estimated duration. In case of an emergency or if you fail to return on time, they will be able to assist or notify the necessary authorities.

6. Carry identification: It's always a good idea to carry some form of identification, such as an ID card or a wristband with emergency contact information. This can be vital in case of an accident or medical emergency. Consider purchasing a ROAD iD, the premier line of safety identification tags and bracelets for runner ID, cyclist ID, medical ID, bicycling ID, and emergency medical ID.

7. Stay hydrated: Proper hydration is essential for your overall well-being and safety while running. Carry a water bottle or plan your route near water fountains where you can refill.

8. Dress appropriately: Wear comfortable, breathable clothing suitable for the weather conditions. In hot weather, opt for light-colored, moisture-wicking fabrics, and in cold weather, layer up to stay warm. Consider wearing a hat and sunscreen to protect yourself from the sun's harmful rays.

Remember that safety should always be your top priority when running outdoors. By following these tips, you can minimize the risks and maximize your enjoyment of this wonderful activity. Stay safe, stay fit, and continue to explore the joy of running!

Running in Different Weather Conditions

Running is a versatile and enjoyable activity that can be done in various weather conditions. Whether it's a sunny day, a rainy afternoon, or a cold winter morning, there are ways to adapt your running routine to suit the weather. This subchapter will provide you with valuable insights on how to run in different weather conditions, ensuring that you stay safe, comfortable, and motivated throughout your jogging journey.

Running in the heat requires special attention to prevent overheating and dehydration. It is crucial to choose the right time of day for your run, preferably early morning or late evening when the temperatures are cooler. Dress in lightweight, breathable clothing, and don't forget to wear a hat and apply sunscreen to protect yourself from the sun's harmful rays. Stay hydrated by drinking water before, during, and after your run, and listen to your body, slowing down or taking breaks when necessary.

Running in the rain can be a refreshing and invigorating experience. To stay comfortable, opt for quick-drying fabrics that wick away moisture and protect your feet with waterproof shoes. Avoid running near lightning or in areas prone to flooding. Embrace the wetness and adjust your pace if needed, as running on slippery surfaces requires extra caution. Remember to dry off and change into dry clothes after your run to avoid getting chilled.

Running in cold weather can be challenging but equally rewarding. Layer your clothing to stay warm, starting with a moisture-wicking base layer, followed by an insulating middle layer, and finally, a windproof and waterproof outer layer. Protect your extremities by wearing gloves, a hat, and warm socks. Warm-up properly indoors before heading out to prevent muscle strains in the cold. Be mindful of icy patches and adjust your stride to maintain stability.

Running in different weather conditions can be an exciting way to vary your routine and challenge yourself. By adapting your attire, being aware of potential hazards, and listening to your body, you can safely enjoy the benefits of running in any weather. Remember to always prioritize your safety and comfort to make the most out of your running experience.

Running in various weather conditions can add diversity to your routine but also requires adaptability. Here's the reader's digest guide to running in different weather:

Warm Weather (Summer)

Stay Hydrated: In high temperatures, dehydration is a concern. Drink plenty of water before, during, and after your run. Time Your Runs: Opt for early mornings or evenings when temperatures are cooler. Avoid peak heat hours to prevent heat-related illnesses.

Cold Weather (Winter)

Layer Up: Dress in layers to trap heat close to your body. A moisture-wicking base layer, an insulating layer, and a windproof outer layer work well. Protect Extremities: Don't forget gloves, a hat, and thermal socks to protect your hands, head, and feet from the cold.

Rainy Weather

Wear Waterproof Gear: Invest in a good-quality waterproof jacket and moisture-wicking clothing. Ensure your shoes provide sufficient grip to prevent slipping. Visibility: Choose brightly colored or reflective clothing to enhance visibility, especially on gloomy days.

Hot and Humid Weather

Light Clothing: Opt for light-colored, breathable fabrics to stay cool. Consider a hat or visor to shield your face from the sun. Sunscreen: Apply sunscreen to exposed skin to prevent sunburn. Sunglasses can protect your eyes from UV rays.

Wind

Dress Windproof: Wind can make the air feel colder. Wear windproof layers, especially on windy days, to maintain warmth. Plan Your Route: Consider starting your run into the wind, so it's at your back on the way home.

Snow and Ice

Traction: Use shoes with good traction or consider adding slip-on traction devices to your shoes. Shorten Strides: Take shorter strides to maintain balance on icy surfaces

Extreme Weather Conditions

Know Your Limits: In extreme conditions, such as storms or excessive heat, consider indoor alternatives to stay safe. Monitor Health: Pay attention to how your body responds to extreme conditions and adjust your intensity accordingly.

Remember to listen to your body, adjust your pace, and prioritize safety in challenging weather conditions. Having the right gear for each situation will ensure you can enjoy running year-round.

Running in different weather conditions can also be an exciting way to vary your routine and challenge yourself. By adapting your attire, being aware of potential hazards, and listening to your body, you can safely enjoy the benefits of running in any weather. Remember to always prioritize your safety and comfort to make the most out of your running experience.

Whether you prefer sunshine, rain, or snow, running is a versatile activity that can be enjoyed in all weather conditions. Embrace the elements, be prepared, and let the weather add an extra dimension to your running routine.

Sharing the Road and Trails with Others

When it comes to running, it's not just about putting one foot in front of the other. It's also about being mindful of the space we share with others. Whether you're running on the road or the trails, it's important to be aware of your surroundings and considerate of fellow runners, walkers, and cyclists. In this subchapter, we will discuss some essential tips for sharing the road and trails with others, ensuring a safe and enjoyable experience for everyone.

First and foremost, always be aware of your surroundings. Pay attention to the people around you, whether they are on foot, on a bike, or in a vehicle. Avoid distractions such as listening to loud music or talking on your phone, as they can hinder your ability to react to potential hazards. By staying alert, you can anticipate and avoid any potential collisions or accidents.

When running on the road, it's crucial to follow the rules of the road. Run against traffic, so you can see approaching vehicles and react accordingly. Use designated pedestrian crossings when available, and always obey traffic signals. Make sure to make yourself visible to drivers, especially in low-light conditions, by wearing reflective clothing or using a headlamp.

On trails, be mindful of other trail users. Yield to pedestrians, especially those with strollers or pets. Announce your presence by saying "passing on your left" or using a bell when approaching others from behind. Maintain a reasonable speed and give ample space when overtaking someone. Remember, trails are for everyone to enjoy, so be respectful and preserve the natural environment by not littering.

When encountering fellow runners, always be friendly and courteous. Offer a smile, a nod, or a simple greeting. It's a great opportunity to connect with others who share the same passion for running. If you see someone struggling, offer words of encouragement. Remember, we're all on this journey together, and supporting each other makes it even more rewarding.

In summary, sharing the road and trails with others requires mindfulness, respect, and good communication. By being aware of your surroundings, following the rules of the road, and being considerate towards fellow runners, walkers, and cyclists, you can ensure a safe and enjoyable experience for everyone. So lace up your running shoes, embrace the camaraderie, and remember that sharing the road and trails is an essential part of the running community.

Finding Your Ideal Jogging or Running Spots

Choosing the right location for your jogging or running routine is a crucial decision that can significantly impact your overall experience. In this section, we'll explore essential factors to consider when finding your ideal jogging or running locations, ensuring a safe, enjoyable, and effective workout. From scenic trails to urban routes, let's navigate the diverse options available to make the most of your running journey.

Selecting an optimal location for jogging or running is vital for a safe and effective workout. It's crucial to choose a place with secure and even terrain, avoiding hills or rough surfaces that could negatively impact your legs and hinder your performance. Opting for a flat and well-maintained area ensures a smoother jogging experience and is particularly beneficial for individuals who may struggle with inclines. Prioritizing safety and comfort, your chosen location should facilitate an easy and paced jogging routine, preventing unnecessary strain and overexertion.

While parks might initially seem like ideal spaces for jogging, it's crucial to exercise caution when selecting one. If a park doubles as a children's playground, the terrain may not be consistently level, making it less than ideal for a jogging trail. Additionally, the presence of playground equipment may obstruct a straight jogging path, which is preferable for a healthy jog. Potential obstacles such as rocks and dirt piles can negatively impact your routine, posing a risk of tripping, stumbling, or falling and increasing the likelihood of injury. Careful consideration of the park's suitability is essential for a safe and effective jogging experience.

When seeking the ideal jogging location, prioritize areas with level and smooth trails. Jogging on rough and uneven terrain not only makes the activity challenging but also increases the risk of injury to your legs and knees. Opt for a surface that strikes a balance, offering firmness without hindering your jogging ability. An ideal solution is a track typically designated for running; however, consider the track's condition, especially after heavy rain or in cold weather. While not everyone has access to a school or college track, or it may not be available to the public, aim to choose a location that replicates the features of such environments as closely as possible.

Embarking on a jogging or running journey offers the opportunity to explore a diverse range of scenic trails and urban routes. Whether you prefer the tranquility of nature or the vibrant energy of city streets, there are options to suit every preference.

Scenic Trails

Forest Trails: Immerse yourself in the serenity of forest trails, surrounded by towering trees and the soothing sounds of nature. These trails often provide a peaceful escape, allowing you to reconnect with the environment.

Coastal Paths: Run along the coastline, enjoying breathtaking views of the sea. Coastal paths offer a refreshing breeze and a visually stunning backdrop that can make your run both invigorating and inspiring.

Mountain Trails: For those seeking a more challenging terrain, mountain trails provide a thrilling experience. Navigate rocky paths and steep inclines while relishing panoramic views from elevated vantage points.

Urban Routes

City Parks: Many cities boast expansive parks that serve as perfect jogging spots. These areas often feature well-maintained paths, green spaces, and sometimes even outdoor fitness equipment.

Riverfronts: Run alongside rivers, enjoying the dynamic cityscape. Riverfront routes provide a blend of urban and natural elements, creating a unique and engaging running environment.

Downtown Streets: Navigate the bustling streets of downtown areas. Running through city centers allows you to absorb the urban energy, pass iconic landmarks, and stay connected with the vibrant pulse of city life.

Tips for Exploration

Plan Ahead: Research different routes in your area or areas you plan to visit. Look for dedicated running trails, parks, or scenic spots.

Stay Safe: Prioritize well-lit areas, especially if running in the early morning or evening. Be aware of your surroundings and adhere to traffic rules if running in urban settings.

Variety is Key: Rotate between scenic trails and urban routes to keep your routine interesting. This variety not only adds excitement but also challenges different muscle groups.

By exploring a mix of scenic and urban running routes, you can customize your experience, keeping your routine dynamic and enjoyable. Whether you seek the peace of nature or the buzz of city life, there's a running path to suit every mood and fitness goal.

Taking Care of the Environment

In the pursuit of a healthy lifestyle, it is important for runners to not only focus on their personal well-being but also consider the health of the environment. As responsible individuals, we have a duty to protect and preserve the natural world around us. This subchapter aims to shed light on the ways in which runners can contribute to taking care of the environment while enjoying their jogging activities.

One of the key aspects of being an environmentally conscious runner is to choose sustainable gear. When selecting running shoes and apparel, look for brands that prioritize eco-friendly materials and production methods. Many companies now offer products made from recycled materials or sustainable fabrics such as bamboo or organic cotton. By making these choices, runners can minimize their carbon footprint and support sustainable practices within the industry.

Another important consideration is the impact of our running routes on the environment. Whenever possible, opt for trails or parks rather than busy city streets. Urban areas not only contribute to air pollution but also have limited green spaces. By exploring natural areas, runners can connect with nature, enjoy cleaner air, and reduce their impact on the environment. Additionally, it is crucial to stay on designated paths to avoid damaging local ecosystems and wildlife habitats.

Water conservation is also essential for environmentally conscious runners. Instead of relying solely on disposable plastic bottles, invest in a reusable water bottle. This small change can significantly reduce plastic waste and help protect our oceans and landfills. Furthermore, when running in parks or nature reserves, be mindful of water sources and avoid contaminating them with waste or pollutants.

Lastly, consider joining or organizing community clean-up events. Running groups can come together to remove litter from running trails or participate in local environmental initiatives. By actively engaging in these activities, runners can positively impact their communities and inspire others to do the same.

Taking care of the environment is not just a responsibility but an opportunity for runners to make a difference. By making conscious choices in our gear, running routes, water consumption, and community involvement, we can contribute to a healthier and more sustainable world. Let us remember that as runners, we are not just jogging for ourselves but for the well-being of the planet we call home.

Chapter 13: Common Running FAQs and Troubleshooting

How Can One Navigate and Overcome Running Plateaus?

One of the most common challenges faced by runners, regardless of their experience level, is the dreaded running plateau. It's that frustrating point in your running journey where you feel like you've hit a wall and can't seem to improve any further. Whether you're a beginner or a seasoned jogger, running plateaus can be demotivating and discouraging. However, it's important to remember that they are a natural part of the process and can be overcome with the right strategies.

First and foremost, it's essential to assess your training routine and make necessary adjustments. Many runners fall into the trap of sticking to the same routine day after day, which can lead to stagnation. To break through a plateau, consider incorporating variety into your workouts. This could involve changing your running route, adding intervals or sprints to your sessions, or trying cross-training activities such as cycling or swimming. By challenging your body with new stimuli, you can break free from the monotony and kickstart your progress.

Additionally, it's crucial to pay attention to your body's signals and adjust your training load accordingly. Sometimes, plateaus occur due to overtraining or not allowing enough time for recovery. If you've been pushing yourself too hard without giving your body enough rest, it may be time to scale back your mileage or intensity for a while. Remember, rest days are just as important as training days, as they allow your muscles to repair and grow stronger.

Another effective strategy to overcome running plateaus is to set new goals. Having a clear objective in mind can reignite your motivation and provide a sense of purpose. Whether it's completing a specific distance, improving your pace, or participating in a race, having a goal to work towards can help you push through plateaus and stay focused on your progress.

Lastly, don't forget to celebrate your achievements along the way, no matter how small they may seem. Running plateaus can be discouraging, but it's important to acknowledge the progress you've already made. Remember that every run, even on plateau days, contributes to your overall fitness and wellbeing.

In conclusion, running plateaus are a common obstacle faced by runners of all levels. By incorporating variety into your training routine, listening to your body, setting new goals, and celebrating your achievements, you can overcome these plateaus and continue progressing on your running journey. Stay persistent, stay motivated, and remember that perseverance is key to becoming the best runner you can be.

How Shin Splints and Joint Pain be Effectively Addressed?

Shin splints and joint pain are common issues that many runners, especially beginners, often encounter. These conditions can be frustrating and discouraging, but with the right knowledge and strategies, they can be addressed effectively. In this subchapter, we will explore some practical tips and techniques to help you overcome these obstacles and continue enjoying your running journey.

Shin splints, also known as medial tibial stress syndrome, refer to the pain and inflammation along the inner edge of the shinbone. This condition is typically caused by overuse or improper running technique. To address shin splints, it is crucial to listen to your body and give it time to heal. Rest and ice the affected area, and consider using compression sleeves or elastic bandages to provide support and reduce inflammation. Gradually ease back into running, incorporating low-impact exercises such as swimming or cycling in the meantime.

Joint pain, on the other hand, can be caused by various factors, such as muscle imbalances, poor form, or worn-out shoes. To alleviate joint pain, it is important to focus on strengthening the muscles surrounding the joints. Incorporate exercises that target the quadriceps, hamstrings, and calves into your training routine. Additionally, ensure that you have proper running shoes that provide adequate cushioning and support for your feet. Consider consulting a professional shoe fitter to find the right pair for your specific needs.

Proper warm-up and cool-down routines are essential for preventing both shin splints and joint pain. Begin each running session with a dynamic warm-up, which includes activities like leg swings, lunges, and high knees. This helps to loosen up the muscles and prepare them for the upcoming workout. After your run, take the time to cool down with static stretches, focusing on the calves, hamstrings, and quadriceps. This will help reduce muscle tightness and minimize the risk of developing pain or injuries.

Lastly, consider incorporating cross-training activities into your routine. Engaging in low-impact exercises, such as swimming, yoga, or cycling, can give your joints a break from the repetitive pounding of running while still providing cardiovascular benefits. This variety in your workouts will not only reduce the risk of overuse injuries but also improve overall fitness and strength.

By taking a proactive approach and implementing these strategies, you can effectively address shin splints and joint pain. Remember, consistency is key, and it's important to listen to your body's signals. With patience and perseverance, you will be able to overcome these obstacles and enjoy a pain-free running experience.

How Can You Modify Your Running Routine to Accommodate Busy Schedules?

In the midst of hectic and busy schedules, adjusting your running routine becomes essential for maintaining a consistent exercise regimen. Between work, family, and other commitments, it's easy for our fitness routines to take a backseat. However, with a little planning and some adjustments, it is possible to maintain a consistent running routine even with a busy schedule. In this subchapter, we will explore some practical strategies to help you fit running into your daily life.

First and foremost, it's essential to prioritize your health and well-being. Recognize the importance of regular exercise and the positive impact it can have on your physical and mental health. By making running a priority, you will be more motivated to find time for it. There are several strategies you can employ to ensure that running remains a feasible and integral part of your routine:

1. Shorten Your Runs: Instead of long, time-consuming runs, consider shortening the duration while maintaining intensity. Break your runs into smaller, more manageable chunks. Instead of trying to find an hour or more for a long run, split it into two shorter runs. For example, you could run 20 minutes in the morning and another 20 minutes in the evening. This approach allows you to still reap the benefits of a longer run while fitting it into your busy schedule. High-intensity interval training (HIIT) can also be an efficient way to achieve cardiovascular significant benefits in a shorter amount of time. By alternating between bursts of intense running and periods of active recovery, you can maximize your workout in as little as 20 minutes.

2. Prioritize Key Workouts: Identify the most crucial workouts in your routine and prioritize them. Focus on key elements such as speed training, endurance runs, or strength workouts to make the most of your limited time.

3. Incorporate Commute Runs: If possible, integrate running into your daily commute. Whether it's running to or from work or incorporating short runs during lunch breaks, this can be an effective way to utilize time that might otherwise be spent commuting. Utilizing your lunch break is another great way to squeeze in a run. If you have access to a nearby park or a gym with shower facilities, consider using your lunch hour to get some exercise. This not only allows you to get your run in but also provides a refreshing break from your workday, boosting your productivity and focus for the afternoon.

4. Early Mornings or Late Evenings: Consider adjusting your running schedule to early mornings or late evenings when your schedule might be less hectic. This can help you carve out dedicated time for running without conflicting with work or other commitments.

5. Utilize Weekends: If weekdays are particularly busy, use weekends for longer runs or more extensive workout sessions. This can compensate for shorter sessions during the week.

6. Combine Exercise with Other Activities: Integrate running with other commitments or activities. For example, you could jog while your child practices sports or run errands on foot to combine exercise with daily tasks. Consider involving your family and friends in your running routine. Try to plan runs with your spouse, children, or friends, making it a social activity. Not only will this help you stay motivated, but it also allows you to spend quality time with loved ones while staying active.

7. Embrace Flexibility: Understand that not every run needs to follow a rigid schedule. Be flexible and adapt your running routine based on the demands of your daily life.

8. Invest in Home Exercise Equipment: Consider investing in a treadmill or other home exercise equipment. This allows you to work out without the time constraints associated with traveling to a gym or running outdoors.

Remember, the key is finding a balance that works for you. By making strategic adjustments and staying flexible, you can successfully integrate running into even the busiest of schedules, ensuring that your physical well-being remains a priority.

Adjusting your running routine for a busy schedule requires commitment and creativity. With proper planning and determination, you can maintain a consistent running routine and enjoy the many benefits it brings to your life, even with a hectic lifestyle.

Is Jogging Safe for Heart Patients?

Engaging in regular physical activity is generally considered beneficial for overall health, including cardiovascular health. However, when it comes to specific activities like jogging for individuals with heart conditions, it's crucial to approach exercise with caution and under the guidance of a healthcare professional.

In some cases, jogging might be contraindicated, especially for individuals with severe heart conditions or those who have recently undergone cardiac procedures. Certain heart conditions, such as unstable angina, severe heart failure, or recent heart attacks, may require more caution and a tailored exercise plan.

For many people with heart conditions, jogging can be safe and even beneficial, as it helps improve cardiovascular fitness, strengthens the heart, and enhances overall well-being. However, it's essential to consider individual factors such as the severity of the heart condition, overall health, and any other existing medical conditions.

While heart patients are often advised to engage in walking, the safety of jogging for them remains a question. The distinction between brisk walking and jogging is minimal, and the key consideration lies in the varying degrees of heart problems among different patients. It is crucial to acknowledge that only the cardiologist possesses a comprehensive understanding of the severity of a patient's condition. While jogging may be suitable for one patient, another may be limited to brisk or even leisurely walking. Ultimately, determining the appropriateness of jogging hinges on understanding the specific stress levels that an individual patient's heart can withstand, a determination that should be made based on the patient's overall health.

Before starting a jogging or any exercise program, individuals with heart conditions should consult with their healthcare provider. The healthcare professional can assess the individual's current health status, review medical history, and recommend an appropriate exercise plan based on individual needs and limitations.

Even if you feel well, it's crucial never to embark on jogging without your doctor's approval. There could be various reasons why your doctor might advise against jogging, particularly if you've undergone heart surgery. Healing takes time, and only your doctor can assess when you're sufficiently healed to engage in jogging. Given that jogging is significantly more strenuous than walking, it's important to refrain from jogging until your doctor gives the green light. Not every exercise, even one as beneficial as jogging, is universally suitable, and engaging in it without proper guidance may potentially lead to health issues rather than contributing to a healthier body.

If your doctor doesn't provide guidance on whether jogging is suitable after a heart attack or surgery, approach it with the same caution as any diet or exercise regimen—consult your doctor before participating. Share your desired exercise routine with your doctor, and await their assessment of its appropriateness for you. If your doctor advises against it, you're entitled to seek clarification but refrain from making independent decisions. Trust your doctor's judgment, as they have access to your complete health records, including EKGs. Even if your doctor suggests a limitation to leisurely walking for the long term, it's essential to accept their recommendation, recognizing that it is made in your best interest.

For those deemed suitable to jog, it's important to start gradually and progress at a pace that allows the body to adapt. Warm-up exercises and cool-down sessions are crucial to prevent injuries and ensure a safe workout. Monitoring for any signs of discomfort, chest pain, or shortness of breath during exercise is essential. If any such symptoms occur, it's crucial to stop exercising immediately and seek medical attention.

Whether or not you've experienced a heart attack, or if you have a heart condition that jogging might impact, it's crucial to consult your doctor before engaging in such activities. Your doctor possesses the knowledge of factors that could influence your heart condition or potentially exacerbate it. Avoid the misconception that jogging is universally healthy, as there are circumstances under which it may not be advisable for everyone. Always seek your doctor's guidance to ensure that any exercise regimen aligns with your specific health needs and conditions.

To sum up, jogging can be safe for heart patients under the right conditions and with proper guidance. Consultation with a healthcare professional is paramount to ensure an individualized exercise plan that aligns with the specific needs and health status of the individual. Regular monitoring, a gradual approach, and staying attuned to one's body are essential components of a safe jogging routine for individuals with heart conditions.

Will Jogging Excasterbate Existing Knee Issues?

Addressing the concern of whether jogging can worsen pre-existing knee issues is crucial for individuals with a history of knee problems. While jogging is a popular form of exercise with various health benefits, it's essential to evaluate its impact on knee health. A lot of information circulates about jogging potentially causing knee problems, but what about individuals who already have existing knee issues? Does jogging worsen their condition, and are there measures to prevent knee problems while engaging in this activity?

One effective way to mitigate the risk of knee problems during jogging is by selecting appropriate footwear. Opting for quality athletic shoes with specific designs tailored for running is crucial. Rather than choosing inexpensive street sneakers from a department store, it's advisable to go for running shoes or even specialized running sneakers, as they provide better support and are designed with the specific needs of jogging in mind. While some may prefer cross-trainer shoes for versatility in various activities, when it comes to jogging, opting for dedicated running shoes is often a better choice.

Engaging in jogging may pose challenges for individuals with bad knees, potentially leading to increased discomfort or exacerbation of existing problems. The repetitive impact and stress on the knee joints during jogging could contribute to pain or further issues. Before incorporating jogging into a fitness routine, particularly for those with a history of knee problems, consulting with a healthcare professional is advisable. They can provide personalized guidance, considering the individual's specific knee condition, overall health, and fitness goals. It's crucial to prioritize joint health and choose exercises that promote overall well-being without risking further damage.

Jogging, if not approached with caution, can potentially exacerbate knee problems, making it a risky choice for those with pre-existing issues. If you're dealing with existing knee issues, alternatives to jogging, like walking may prove to be a more suitable option due to the reduced stress on the knees. While it might not align exactly with your preferences, the choice between walking and jogging becomes essential to prevent additional damage. Making the wrong decision could lead to the need for knee surgery, and there's no guarantee that the problem will be permanently resolved.

Some individuals who take up jogging despite having knee issues may discover that their problems worsen. This is often a result of the stress placed on the knees during jogging. Additionally, wearing poorly fitting shoes, particularly from a time when sneakers were the predominant athletic footwear, can contribute to knee problems. During that era, specialized running shoes were not available, and athletic footwear was primarily designed for sports like football, basketball, baseball, and golf. Running shoes are a relatively recent addition to the market compared to the extensive history of jogging and track activities. As a result, individuals experiencing knee issues related to jogging are often older individuals who began jogging before the advent of running shoes or before awareness of their significance. Today, many of these individuals face challenges such as knee and calf problems, making it difficult for some to venture beyond their homes or visit stores.

Whether jogging exacerbates existing knee issues depends on individual factors. Seeking professional advice and considering alternative exercises can help individuals make informed decisions about their fitness routines while safeguarding their knee health.

Should You Jog When You're Pregnant?

The decision to jog during pregnancy is a personal one and should be made in consultation with your healthcare provider. Generally, exercise during pregnancy is encouraged as it can provide numerous benefits, such as improved mood, reduced back pain, and enhanced stamina. However, jogging specifically requires careful consideration due to its impact on the joints and the potential for an increased heart rate.

While doctors often advise pregnant patients to engage in exercise, the question of whether jogging is a suitable option depends largely on whether the individual was jogging before becoming pregnant. In most cases, doctors recommend that pregnant patients continue exercises they were doing before pregnancy rather than starting new ones. However, this decision is contingent on factors such as the mother-to-be's weight, age, and overall health, and it's a decision best made in consultation between the patient and their doctor. Various reasons, specific to the individual's health and pregnancy, may prompt a doctor to advise against jogging. Therefore, it is crucial not to assume that continuing jogging during pregnancy is safe without consulting with a doctor first.

Before engaging in jogging or any exercise routine during pregnancy, it is essential to consult with your obstetrician or healthcare provider. They can assess your individual health, any pre-existing conditions, and the specific details of your pregnancy to determine whether jogging is a safe and suitable activity for you.

In some cases, jogging may be contraindicated, especially for women with certain pregnancy complications, such as preterm labor, preeclampsia, or a history of recurrent pregnancy loss. Additionally, if you experience dizziness, shortness of breath, chest pain, or any unusual symptoms while jogging, it's crucial to stop immediately and seek medical advice.

Jogging involves a slow, rhythmic gait, and in many cases, pregnant women may participate as long as their doctor approves. However, as the pregnancy progresses, it may become more challenging, potentially leading to the bouncing of the tummy and affecting the baby. When selecting exercise during pregnancy, it's important to be cautious and sensible. Walking is always a safe alternative, and if jogging is not feasible or not permitted by your doctor, walking remains a healthy option.

While jogging has its benefits, it's crucial not to override your doctor's advice. If your healthcare provider advises against jogging during pregnancy, it's essential to respect that decision. Your doctor understands the specifics of your pregnancy, and putting faith in their recommendations is key. It's only a temporary adjustment for a few months, and after your pregnancy, you can resume your jogging routine.

If your healthcare provider approves jogging during pregnancy, it's important to modify your routine to ensure safety. This may include adjusting the intensity and duration and choosing appropriate terrain to minimize the impact on your joints. Staying well-hydrated and wearing supportive athletic shoes are also essential considerations.

Pregnant women who were avid joggers before pregnancy may find it beneficial to transition to lower-impact exercises, such as brisk walking, swimming, or prenatal yoga, as their pregnancy progresses. These activities can provide cardiovascular benefits without placing excessive stress on the joints.

During the early stages of pregnancy, participating in jogging is likely safe. However, as your stomach swells, attempting to jog may become uncomfortable. The increasing bulge may make walking, let alone jogging, less comfortable. It's important to note that exercise during pregnancy contributes to smoother labor, so if jogging becomes impractical, don't let it deter you from walking. Staying active and limber is crucial for an easier delivery. Nevertheless, it's essential to choose activities that won't pose risks to the baby or the pregnancy. Always prioritize following your doctor's advice to ensure a safe and healthy pregnancy journey.

Ultimately, the decision to jog during pregnancy should be an informed one, taking into account your individual health, the progression of your pregnancy, and the guidance of your healthcare provider. Regular communication with your healthcare team ensures that your exercise routine aligns with the unique needs and circumstances of your pregnancy.

Does Jogging or Running Offer Health Benefits for Everyone?

The question of whether jogging or running provides health benefits for everyone is an important consideration. While these forms of exercise are renowned for their positive impact on cardiovascular health, endurance, and overall well-being, the extent to which they benefit individuals can vary. Several factors come into play, including age, fitness levels, existing health conditions, and personal preferences.

Jogging and running are generally considered effective ways to enhance cardiovascular fitness, maintain a healthy weight, and reduce the risk of various chronic conditions. However, it's crucial to recognize that individuals differ in their physical capabilities and health statuses.

Although many people are physically capable of jogging, it is always advisable to consult with a healthcare professional if you have any underlying health concerns that might make jogging or running unsafe for you. Making the right choice is crucial, as jogging or running undertaken without consideration of your health condition may not contribute to improvements and could, in fact, be counterproductive.

For some, jogging may be a suitable and enjoyable exercise, contributing to improved fitness levels and mental well-being. However, others may find running more appropriate, as it allows for a higher-intensity workout and increased calorie expenditure.

Those unable to engage in running or brisk walking, particularly those with back, knee, or leg problems, might want to reconsider participating in jogging. The additional stress from jogging could potentially exacerbate existing problems. However, this doesn't mean individuals with such conditions should avoid exercise altogether. Instead, they should opt for activities recommended by their doctor, taking into account their specific condition.

Certain health considerations, such as joint health and pre-existing medical conditions, may influence the suitability of jogging or running for specific individuals. Individuals with joint issues might prefer low-impact exercises, while those with certain medical conditions may need to consult with healthcare professionals before engaging in vigorous physical activity.

Engaging in an activity that exceeds the body's capacity can lead to additional health issues. The key is making choices that align with individual capabilities, allowing for the continuation of an active lifestyle. Making informed decisions prevents the risk of compromising one's ability to perform activities they once enjoyed. It's crucial to recognize personal limitations and accept them rather than attempting to surpass them and potentially face negative consequences.

In our youth, we were resilient, overcoming limitations without letting anything bring us down. However, as we age, it becomes essential to navigate around these limitations. This involves avoiding activities that are impossible or may cause injury, such as jogging, which may no longer be feasible. Instead, there are alternative activities like brisk or leisurely walking that can be pursued. It's crucial not to put undue stress on the body, especially after procedures like knee surgery. Being reasonable about our capabilities ensures that there are plenty of aerobic exercises available for anyone interested in improving their health without risking injury.

Ultimately, the question of whether jogging or running is beneficial for everyone underscores the importance of individualized approaches to fitness. Before starting any exercise regimen, particularly jogging or running, it is advisable to consult with a healthcare provider or fitness professional. A personalized assessment can help determine the most appropriate exercise plan based on an individual's health status, fitness goals, and overall well-being.

Finding Support and Resources for Runners

Running is not just a physical activity; it is a lifestyle that requires dedication and support. Whether you are a beginner or an experienced runner, having access to the right resources and support can make a significant difference in your running journey. In this subchapter, we will explore various avenues that can help you find the support and resources you need to excel in your running endeavors.

One of the first places to start is with local running clubs and communities. These groups are a treasure trove of knowledge and experience, providing you with the opportunity to connect with like-minded individuals who share your passion for running. Joining a running club not only offers camaraderie but also provides access to group runs, training programs, and expert advice from seasoned runners.

Another invaluable resource for runners is online platforms and forums. Websites dedicated to running, social media groups, and online forums are excellent places to seek advice, gain insights, and connect with runners from around the world. These platforms are especially beneficial for beginners as they can find answers to common questions, seek training plans, and receive motivation from the running community.

Running specialty stores are also fantastic places to find support and resources for runners. These stores have knowledgeable staff who can guide you in selecting the right running shoes, clothing, and accessories. They often host clinics, workshops, and events that cater to runners of all levels, providing opportunities to learn from experts and interact with fellow runners.

Additionally, consider seeking support from professional coaches or trainers. These individuals possess expertise in developing customized training plans, improving running form, and preventing injuries. Hiring a coach or trainer can help you maximize your potential and achieve your running goals more effectively.

Lastly, do not underestimate the power of books, podcasts, and other educational resources dedicated to running. These materials can offer valuable insights, training tips, and inspiration to keep you motivated and informed. From memoirs of legendary runners to instructional guides on proper nutrition and injury prevention, there is an abundance of resources available to help you on your running journey.

Runners have access to a wealth of support and resources to enhance their running experience, from training programs to online communities. Here's the **reader's digest guide** to the various types of support and resources available for runners:

1. Running Clubs and Communities: Joining a running club or online community provides a sense of camaraderie and support. Local running clubs often organize group runs, offer coaching, and provide a supportive environment for runners of all levels.

2. Coaching Programs: Professional coaches and coaching programs can offer personalized training plans, guidance on technique, and insights into optimizing your running performance. Whether you're a beginner or aiming for a specific goal, a coach can provide valuable support.

3. Running Apps: Numerous running apps are designed to track your runs, provide training plans, and offer motivation. Apps like Strava, Nike Run Club, and Couch to 5K can help you stay on track and connect with a broader running community.

4. Online Training Platforms: Platforms like Garmin Connect, TrainingPeaks, Strava, and MapMyRun allow you to log and analyze your runs, track progress, and set goals. Many of these platforms offer advanced features for more serious athletes.

5. Nutritional Guidance: Proper nutrition is crucial for runners. Seek resources or consult with nutritionists who specialize in sports nutrition to optimize your diet for performance, recovery, and overall well-being.

6. Footwear and Gear Expertise: Visit specialty running stores for expert advice on choosing the right running shoes and gear. The knowledgeable staff can analyze your gait, recommend suitable footwear, and help prevent injuries associated with improper gear.

7. Physical Therapists and Injury Prevention: Injuries are a common concern for runners. Physical therapists can offer guidance on injury prevention, rehabilitation exercises, and recovery strategies. Regular check-ins can help address potential issues before they become serious.

8. Race Events and Organizations: Participate in organized races and events to challenge yourself and experience the excitement of the running community. Race organizations often provide training plans, race-day support, and post-race festivities.

9. Educational Resources: Books, podcasts, and online articles abound with valuable information on running techniques, training methodologies, and inspirational stories. Stay informed about the latest research and trends in running through reputable sources.

10. Supportive Friends and Family: Share your running journey with friends and family who provide encouragement and support. Having a strong support system can make a significant difference in staying motivated and committed.

11. Mental Health Resources: Running is not just about physical health; mental well-being is equally important. Explore resources on mindfulness, stress management, and the mental benefits of running to maintain a healthy balance.

12. Local Running Events and Meetups: Attend local running events, meetups, or charity runs to connect with other runners in your area. These gatherings foster a sense of community and may introduce you to new training partners.

13. Online Challenges and Virtual Runs: Engage in online challenges or virtual runs to set and achieve goals, connect with a global running community, and stay motivated. Virtual events offer flexibility and inclusivity for runners of all abilities.

By tapping into these diverse support and resource channels, runners can enrich their experience, overcome challenges, and continuously improve their performance and well-being. Finding support and resources for runners is essential for all individuals, regardless of their running experience. Remember, running is not just about putting one foot in front of the other; it is a collective journey that can be greatly enriched through the support of others and the resources available to you.

Chapter 14: Taking Your Running to the Next Level
Advanced Training Techniques for Experienced Runners

Congratulations on progressing from a beginner to an experienced runner! As you continue your running journey, it's important to challenge yourself and take your training to the next level. In this subchapter, we will explore some advanced training techniques that will help you improve your speed, endurance, and overall performance as an experienced runner.

Interval Training: One effective technique for experienced runners is interval training. This involves alternating between high-intensity sprints and periods of active recovery. For example, you can sprint at maximum effort for 30 seconds, followed by a 1-minute jog to recover. Repeat this cycle for several sets. Interval training helps increase your anaerobic capacity, improves speed, and boosts overall cardiovascular fitness.

Hill Repeats: Incorporating hill repeats into your training can significantly enhance your running strength and power. Find a steep hill and run up it at a challenging pace, then jog or walk back down to recover. Repeat this process for a specific number of sets or a set time. Hill repeats build leg and core strength, improve running form, and simulate race conditions, making you a more efficient runner.

Tempo Runs: Tempo runs are longer runs at a sustained, comfortably hard pace, just below your maximum effort. By running at this pace for an extended period, you train your body to maintain a faster speed over longer distances. Tempo runs improve both speed and endurance, helping you maintain a steady pace during races or longer runs.

Fartlek Training: Fartlek, which means "speed play" in Swedish, is a versatile training technique that involves varying your pace throughout your run. During a fartlek run, you can alternate between sprinting, jogging, and running at different speeds for different distances. This technique helps improve your overall running performance, as it challenges your body to adapt to various intensities and speeds.

Cross-Training: As an experienced runner, it's essential to include cross-training in your routine. Incorporating activities such as swimming, cycling, strength training, or yoga can help prevent overuse injuries, improve overall fitness, and strengthen muscles that running alone may not target. Cross-training also adds variety to your workouts and keeps you motivated.

Remember, as you embark on advanced training techniques, it's crucial to listen to your body and gradually increase the intensity and duration of your workouts. Always warm up before each session, stretch afterward, and allow for adequate rest and recovery time. By incorporating these advanced training techniques into your routine, you'll continue to challenge yourself, reach new milestones, and become an even stronger and more accomplished runner.

Exploring Trail Running and Ultramarathons

Trail running and ultramarathons offer a thrilling and challenging experience for runners looking to take their skills to the next level. In this subchapter of "Running Made Simple: A Beginner's Guide to Jogging and the Basics of Running," we will delve into the world of trail running and ultramarathons, providing valuable insights and tips to help both beginners and seasoned runners excel in this niche.

Trail running is a form of running that takes place on unpaved paths, often in natural environments such as mountains, forests, or deserts. It offers a refreshing change of scenery from the typical road or treadmill runs, allowing runners to connect with nature while pushing their limits. However, trail running requires additional skills and preparation compared to conventional road running.

One of the essential aspects of trail running is selecting the right gear. Unlike road running, where a good pair of running shoes suffices, trail runners need shoes with better traction, stability, and protection against rocks and uneven terrain. Additionally, investing in proper moisture-wicking clothing, a hydration pack, and a light source for night runs is crucial for a successful trail running experience.

Ultramarathons, on the other hand, are races that exceed the traditional marathon distance of 26.2 miles. They can range from 30 miles to over 100 miles and often take place on trails, challenging runners both mentally and physically. Training for an ultramarathon requires a progressive build-up of distance, as well as incorporating strength and endurance exercises into your routine.

To successfully tackle an ultramarathon, it is vital to develop a strategic race plan. This includes setting achievable goals, understanding the course terrain, and practicing proper nutrition and hydration strategies. Moreover, mental fortitude and a positive mindset play a significant role in overcoming the unique challenges that ultramarathons present.

Whether you are a beginner looking to venture into trail running or an experienced runner aiming for an ultramarathon, it is crucial to start gradually and listen to your body. Building a solid foundation of endurance, strength, and technique is essential to prevent injuries and improve performance.

Trail running and ultramarathons introduce a unique set of new challenges and considerations. Here are essential tips to enhance your experience and success in these adventurous pursuits:

1. Gradual Progression: Transitioning to trail running and ultramarathons requires a gradual increase in mileage and difficulty. Begin with shorter trails and progressively tackle more challenging terrains as your strength and endurance improve.

2. Terrain-Specific Training: Train on surfaces and terrains similar to those you'll encounter during trail races. This includes uphill and downhill running, technical trails, and varying types of surfaces like gravel, dirt, and rocks.

3. Proper Footwear: Invest in trail running shoes with adequate grip, support, and protection. The terrain can be unpredictable, and the right footwear can prevent slips, provide stability, and protect your feet from rocks and roots.

4. Hydration and Nutrition: Trail running and ultramarathons often take place in remote locations with limited aid stations. Carry a hydration system and plan your nutrition strategy. Portable snacks, energy gels, and electrolyte supplements are essential for sustained energy.

5. Navigation Skills: Trails may not be as well-marked as roads. Develop basic navigation skills, carry a map or use a GPS device, and be aware of trail markings. Familiarize yourself with the course beforehand to reduce the risk of getting lost.

6. Gear for Changing Weather: Trail running exposes you to various weather conditions. Pack lightweight, weather-appropriate gear, such as a rain jacket, hat, and gloves. Dress in layers to accommodate temperature changes.

7. Respect Nature and Wildlife: Trail runners often venture into natural habitats. Respect the environment, follow Leave No Trace principles, and avoid disturbing wildlife. Stay on marked trails to minimize impact.

8. Strength Training: Develop strength in your legs, core, and stabilizing muscles. This is crucial for navigating uneven terrain, steep ascents, and descents. Incorporate strength training exercises into your routine to enhance overall stability.

9. Practice Downhill Running: Downhill running can be challenging and places additional stress on muscles. Practice downhill running techniques, including shortening your stride, maintaining control, and using your arms for balance.

10. Mental Toughness: Ultramarathons, especially on challenging trails, demand mental resilience. Prepare for moments of fatigue and self-doubt. Develop mental strategies, such as positive self-talk and focusing on small milestones, to overcome challenges.

11. Proper Recovery: Trail running and ultramarathons exert considerable stress on the body. Prioritize recovery with adequate rest, stretching, and recovery tools like foam rolling. Listen to your body and address any signs of injury promptly.

12. Participate in Shorter Trail Races First: Before attempting an ultramarathon, participate in shorter trail races to gain experience and build confidence. These races will help you familiarize yourself with trail conditions and refine your race-day strategies.

13. Know the Course and Elevation: Study the course map and elevation profile. Knowing where steep climbs, technical sections, and aid stations are located allows you to plan your pacing and nutrition accordingly.

14. Socialize and Learn from Experienced Trail Runners: Join trail running groups, attend events, and connect with experienced trail runners. Learning from their experiences and insights can provide valuable tips and enhance your understanding of trail running dynamics.

15. Emergency Preparedness: Trail running may take you to remote areas. Carry a basic first aid kit, know how to use it, and inform someone about your running plans. Be prepared for unexpected situations and changes in weather.

By incorporating these tips into your training and race-day preparations, you'll be better equipped to tackle the challenges of trail running and ultramarathons and enjoy the unique rewards these endeavors offer.

In conclusion, trail running and ultramarathons offer exciting opportunities for runners to explore new challenges and connect with nature. By understanding the specific requirements of these activities and incorporating proper training, gear, and mental preparation, runners of all levels can embark on successful trail running and ultramarathon journeys. So, lace up your trail shoes, embrace the adventure, and push your limits in the exhilarating world of trail running and ultramarathons!

Joining Running Clubs and Communities

Running is not just an individual sport – it can also be a social activity that brings people together. Joining running clubs and communities is a fantastic way to connect with like-minded individuals, find support, and enhance your overall running experience. In this subchapter, we will explore the benefits of joining running clubs and communities, how to find the right one for you, and what to expect when you become part of a running group.

One of the primary advantages of joining a running club is the sense of camaraderie and motivation you will gain. Running with others who share your passion can boost your enthusiasm, provide encouragement, and keep you accountable to your goals. Being part of a community can help you stay motivated, especially when you are facing challenges or experiencing a plateau in your progress.

Running clubs and communities often organize group runs, which can offer a range of benefits. Not only do group runs provide a sense of security and safety, but they also offer an opportunity to explore new routes and discover hidden gems in your local area. Additionally, running with others can help improve your technique, as you can learn from more experienced runners and receive valuable advice and feedback.

Finding the right running club or community is essential to ensure a positive experience. Start by researching local running clubs and communities in your area. Consider factors such as location, meeting times, and the types of runners they cater to. Some clubs may focus on beginners or specific age groups, while others may be more competitive or offer specialized training programs. Attend a few trial runs or events to gauge the atmosphere and see if it aligns with your preferences and abilities.

Once you have found a suitable running club or community, expect to become part of a supportive network. You will meet new friends who share your passion for running and can offer guidance and support along your journey. Many running clubs also organize social events, workshops, and races, which can provide opportunities for personal growth and a deeper connection with the community.

Joining running clubs and communities can significantly enhance your running experience and contribute to your overall well-being. Here are some compelling reasons to consider becoming a part of these groups:

1. Motivation and Accountability: Running clubs provide a supportive environment where members motivate each other to stay consistent with their running routines. The group dynamic creates a sense of accountability, making it more likely for individuals to stick to their training plans.

2. Social Connection: Running is often considered a solitary activity, but joining a running club introduces a social component. You'll have the opportunity to connect with like-minded individuals who share a passion for running. Building friendships within the running community can make your training sessions more enjoyable.

3. Training Support and Advice: Experienced runners within the club can offer valuable insights and advice on training techniques, injury prevention, and race strategies. Whether you're a novice or a seasoned runner, the collective knowledge of the group can enhance your understanding of running principles.

4. Structured Group Runs: Running clubs organize group runs, providing a structured and supportive setting for members to train together. These group runs can vary in intensity and distance, catering to runners of different levels. It's an excellent way to diversify your training and explore new routes.

5. Access to Events and Races: Many running clubs organize or participate in local races and events. Joining a club can give you access to exclusive race opportunities, team relays, and other running-related activities. Participating in events as part of a club fosters a sense of camaraderie and shared achievement.

6. Mental Health Benefits: Running clubs contribute to mental well-being by creating a positive and supportive community. Sharing experiences, triumphs, and challenges with fellow runners can reduce stress, boost mood, and create a sense of belonging.

7. Expert Guidance and Coaching: Some running clubs offer coaching services or have experienced members who can provide guidance on improving running techniques, setting realistic goals, and overcoming obstacles. Access to knowledgeable mentors can significantly accelerate your progress.

8. Diversity and Inclusivity: Running clubs often welcome individuals of all fitness levels, ages, and backgrounds. This diversity creates an inclusive atmosphere where everyone feels encouraged to participate, regardless of their running experience or abilities.

9. Exclusive Discounts and Perks: Many running clubs have partnerships with local running stores, race organizers, and other fitness-related businesses. Joining a club might grant you access to exclusive discounts on running gear, race registrations, and other perks.

10. Community Outreach and Volunteering: Running clubs frequently engage in community outreach and volunteering activities. Participating in such initiatives allows you to give back to the community, fostering a sense of purpose and contributing to the positive image of runners.

11. Inspiration and Goal Setting: Being surrounded by dedicated runners can inspire you to set and achieve ambitious goals. Whether it's completing a marathon, improving your pace, or trying new race distances, the collective enthusiasm within the club can fuel your aspirations.

12. Access to Resources and Information: Running clubs often share valuable resources, including training plans, nutrition tips, and injury prevention strategies. The exchange of information within the group can help you stay informed about the latest developments in the running community.

Joining a running club or community is not only about improving your running skills but also about embracing a lifestyle that prioritizes fitness, friendship, and personal growth. Check local listings, online platforms, or community bulletin boards to find a running club that aligns with your goals and interests. Whether you are a beginner or an experienced runner, being part of a running group can take your running journey to new heights. So lace up your shoes, reach out, and join the vibrant community of runners waiting to welcome you with open arms.

Inspiring Stories of Successful Runners

In this subchapter, we will delve into the inspiring stories of successful runners who have overcome obstacles, pushed their limits, and achieved remarkable feats through their dedication to running. These stories will serve as a motivation for all readers, regardless of their running experience, to strive for greatness and unlock their full potential on the track or the trail.

1. The Comeback Kid: Sarah Johnson

Sarah Johnson's narrative epitomizes the tenacity and grit that define a true athlete. When a severe knee injury cast doubt on her running future, skeptics predicted an end to her running career. Yet, Sarah was unwilling to concede defeat. With a commitment to overcoming the odds, she delved into intensive rehabilitation, demonstrating unparalleled resilience. Not only did she reclaim her status as a runner, but Sarah elevated her achievements to the pinnacle of success, earning the title of a marathon champion. Her journey becomes a beacon of inspiration, underscoring the potency of determination and the indispensable value of unwavering commitment to our aspirations, especially when confronted with formidable challenges. Sarah Johnson's story stands as a testament to the triumph of the human spirit and its ability to surmount adversity on the path to achieving one's goals.

2. From Couch to 5K: Mark Davis

Mark Davis, a former self-proclaimed couch potato, found himself at a crossroads, grappling with weight issues and a sedentary lifestyle. Determined to turn his life around, he took the transformative step of lacing up his running shoes. Mark's journey commenced with small strides, transitioning from walking to slow jogging. With persistent effort, he steadily enhanced his overall fitness, ultimately venturing into the realm of running. His breakthrough came when he successfully completed his inaugural 5K race. Mark, now an emblem of inspiration for novices, showcases that anyone can evolve into a proficient runner through dedication and regularity. His journey has extended to conquering multiple half marathons and achieving the impressive milestone of two full marathons. Mark's story serves as a testament to the incredible potential within every individual to overcome inertia and emerge triumphant in the realm of running.

3. Breaking Barriers: Rachel Thompson

Rachel Thompson stands as a beacon of inspiration for female runners everywhere. In a small rural community, she fearlessly challenged societal norms by becoming the first woman to conquer a full marathon. Rachel's path was laden with difficulties, as she encountered skepticism and criticism. Undeterred, her unshakable self-belief and determination fueled her journey to realizing her dream. Her narrative powerfully underscores the idea that running transcends gender boundaries, emphasizing that with passion and steadfast resolve, anyone can reach the pinnacle of greatness. Rachel's story serves as a rallying call for breaking barriers and forging ahead in the pursuit of one's aspirations, leaving an enduring impact on the running community and beyond.

4. Overcoming Obstacles: James Carter

James Carter's journey is a remarkable testament to the indomitable human spirit. Confronted with a congenital disability affecting his leg muscles, James encountered a series of formidable physical challenges from a young age. Despite these hurdles, his passion for running and an unwavering determination to defy the limitations imposed by his disability propelled him to achieve the status of a Paralympic champion. James's narrative serves as a poignant reminder that armed with the proper mindset and an unyielding will, we possess the capacity to triumph over any obstacle that looms in our path. His story is a beacon of inspiration, illustrating the extraordinary possibilities that unfold when resilience meets ambition.

5. Defying the Odds: William Scott

Scott's running odyssey commenced at the age of 55, marking a resurgence after a two-decade hiatus. Rediscovering the simple joy of running, he progressed from casual jogs to conquering 5Ks, 10Ks, and half marathons. As his 59th birthday approached, Scott harbored a bold ambition – to complete a full marathon before turning 60. With dedicated training, he turned this aspiration into reality. However, the toll of years dedicated to running, training, and racing, compounded by the effects of aging, manifested in knee issues. Facing the challenge head-on, Scott underwent two full knee replacements, receiving advice from doctors to refrain from running. True to his indomitable spirit, Scott embarked on a personal rehabilitation journey, gradually reintroducing himself to the joy of jogging. While he no longer participates in races or extensive runs, Scott finds solace and fulfillment in the daily jogs shared with his two faithful canine companions. His saga is a testament to the enduring love for running and the resilience that transcends physical limitations, proving that the passion for the sport can evolve and endure even in the face of adversity.

In conclusion, these inspiring stories of successful runners highlight the power of determination, perseverance, and self-belief. They prove that running is not only a physical activity but also a transformative journey that can change lives. Whether you are a beginner or an experienced runner, these stories will motivate you to lace up your shoes, hit the pavement, and chase after your own running dreams. Remember, the only limits that exist are the ones we set for ourselves.

Chapter 15: Conclusion - Your Journey as a Runner Begins Now

Congratulations! You have reached the end of "Running Made Simple: A Beginner's Guide to Jogging and the Basics of Running," and your journey as a runner is about to begin. Whether you are a complete novice or someone who wants to get back into running after a long break, this book has equipped you with the essential knowledge and tools to start your running adventure.

Running is not just a physical activity; it is a lifestyle that promotes overall health and well-being. By lacing up your running shoes and hitting the pavement, you are embarking on a path that will transform your body, mind, and spirit. The benefits of running are countless, ranging from improved cardiovascular fitness and weight management to reduced stress and increased mental clarity.

Now that you have learned the fundamentals of running, it's time to put them into practice. Remember, the most important aspect of running is consistency. Start with short distances and gradually increase your mileage over time. Don't push yourself too hard in the beginning; listen to your body and allow it to adapt to the new demands you are placing upon it.

Set realistic goals for yourself. Maybe you want to participate in a local 5K race or complete a half marathon. Whatever your aspirations may be, break them down into smaller, achievable targets. Celebrate each milestone you reach, as these small victories will keep you motivated and committed to your running journey.

As you progress as a runner, don't forget to prioritize self-care. Stretch before and after each run, and incorporate strength training exercises into your routine to prevent injuries. Proper nutrition and hydration are also crucial for optimal performance and recovery.

Additionally, surround yourself with a supportive community of fellow runners. Join a local running group or connect with like-minded individuals online. Sharing your experiences, challenges, and triumphs with others who understand the joys and struggles of running will undoubtedly enhance your journey.

Lastly, always remember to have fun! Running is not just about reaching the finish line; it's about enjoying the process and embracing the freedom and exhilaration that comes with each stride. So, lace up your shoes, take a deep breath, and let the rhythm of your feet carry you forward.

Your journey as a runner begins now. Embrace the challenges, relish the victories, and discover the incredible potential that lies within you. Happy running!

References and Resources

Without Limits® Coaching and Nutrition - www.iamwithoutlimits.com

The coaching program by Without Limits®, is a proven and reliable system tailored to your position in the training journey. They are firm believers that anyone can transform into an athlete. Supported by scientific principles, their coaching approach is customized to align with your specific athletic goals, no matter how big or small, and irrespective of where you are in life. Whether it's endurance coaching or nutrition guidance, they provide excellent comprehensive packages

Runners Essentials by Without Limits® - www.runners-essentials.com

Targeted nutrition for runners and endurance athletes. Physician, Elite Athlete and Nutritionist formulated. A synergy of science, athletics and nutrition.

Bombas Socks - www.shop.bombas.com
Moisture-wicking and odor-resistant alpaca running socks.

Garmin GPS Watches - www.garmin.com
The metrics you need for epic performance.

ROAD iD - www.roadid.com

ROAD iD is the premier line of safety identification tags and bracelets for runner ID, cyclist ID, medical ID, bicycling ID, and emergency medical ID

The Jogging Guide - Indigital Publishing

About the Author

Shawn Tunis's journey into the world of running is a testament to the transformative power of this endurance sport. Unlike many seasoned runners, Shawn's introduction to running was initially associated with punishment during her high school field hockey days, consisting of running laps around the field for late arrivals to practice and for losing games. It wasn't until a significant life change, the birth of her twins in 2011, that her perspective on running underwent a radical shift.

After her pregnancy with twins brought about substantial changes to her body, Shawn embraced running not just as a means to shed post-pregnancy weight but as a personal odyssey to reclaim comfort within her own skin. Her running journey commenced with light jogging, and pushing a double stroller while navigating the challenges of early motherhood. Transitioning from casual jogging to slow running, she discovered an unexpected joy and motivation in the rhythm of her strides.

Driven by her newfound passion, Shawn boldly registered for a 5k race within just two months of taking up running. Despite a challenging first race experience, she remained undeterred. Instead, she persevered, participating in more 5ks and 10ks throughout that pivotal year. Remarkably, within the same year she embarked on her running journey, Shawn completed her first half marathon—a remarkable achievement for any runner.

Unyielding in her pursuit, Shawn's dedication reached its pinnacle the following spring when she triumphantly crossed the finish line of her first marathon. Her journey from viewing running as punishment to embracing it as a source of empowerment showcases the incredible transformation that can unfold when one discovers the physical and mental benefits of this sport. Today, Shawn Tunis stands, not only as an avid runner, but as a testament to the resilience and determination that defines a true runner's spirit.

Her foray into running was not solely driven by the desire to compete but was rather an escape—a personal sanctuary amidst the demands of daily life. For Shawn, running evolved into more than just a physical activity; it became a cherished ritual, offering respite from the routine and a space for personal reflection.

While participating in races remained optional for her, the allure of challenging herself and embracing new experiences led Shawn to explore the world of organized running events. These races, be they 5ks or 10ks, became platforms for personal growth and milestones in her evolving journey as a runner.

The great outdoors became Shawn's preferred arena, where she reveled in the invigorating embrace of fresh air and the rhythmic cadence of her footsteps on the pavement. This connection with nature not only amplified the physical benefits of running, but also contributed to the mental and emotional solace it provided.

A significant chapter in Shawn's running narrative involved the companionship of her twins, sharing the joy of movement and discovery. Pushing them in their double stroller was a mutually enjoyed experience until their growing size and weight made it impractical. Despite this change, the memories forged during those early runs lingered, and the love for running persisted.

Shawn's running journey is not just about crossing finish lines but is a tale of finding solace, embracing challenges, and creating shared moments with her family. It underscores the multifaceted rewards that running can bring—an amalgamation of physical well-being, personal fulfillment, and the joy of shared experiences.

Shawn persevered in her running journey, dedicating years to consistent training under the guidance of a coach. She transformed numerous 5Ks, 10Ks, and half-marathons into stepping stones, each serving as a training ground for the grandeur of completing ten full marathons.

Today, her relationship with running has evolved beyond the structured regimen of training cycles and race goals. Instead, Shawn finds pure joy in the simplicity of running for life, accompanied by the loyal companionship of her dogs. This phase represents a harmonious culmination of her running story—a testament to the enduring passion that fuels her every stride.

You may have heard about the sensation known as the "runner's high." Words may fall short in capturing its essence, but armed with this book as your compass, you might embark on a personal odyssey—from jogging to running—and, with any luck, encounter this extraordinary experience yourself.

Wishing you many happy strides in your running endeavors!